Updating!

Updating!

How to Get a Man or Woman Who
Once Seemed Out of Your League

Leil Lowndes

McGraw·Hill

New York   Chicago   San Francisco   Lisbon   London   Madrid   Mexico City
Milan   New Delhi   San Juan   Seoul   Singapore   Sydney   Toronto

Library of Congress Cataloging-in-Publication Data

Lowndes, Leil.
    Updating! : how to get a man or woman who once seemed out of your league /
Leil Lowndes.
        p.   cm.
    ISBN 0-07-140309-4
    1. Man-woman relationships.   2. Dating (Social customs)   I. Title.

HQ801 .L68   2003
646.7′7—dc21   2003011454

1 2 3 4 5 6 7 8 9 0   AGM/AGM   2 1 0 9 8 7 6 5 4 3

ISBN 0-07-140309-4

McGraw-Hill books are available at special quantity discounts to use as premiums and
sales promotions, or for use in corporate training programs. For more information,
please write to the Director of Special Sales, Professional Publishing, McGraw-Hill, Two
Penn Plaza, New York, NY 10121-2298. Or contact your local bookstore.

This book is printed on acid-free paper.

 Contents

♡ Introduction

How many times have you sat in a restaurant staring at your partner and thinking to yourself, "What am I doing with this . . . *frog*?" Perhaps you justified it by saying, "There's nobody interesting in this town" or "I don't meet any exciting men/women in my job" or "All the good ones are taken."

Or maybe you masochistically attributed it to your own assumed shortcomings. Gentlemen, while dining with your dud date, you sneak a peek at the knockout who's coyly conversing with her date at the next table and you grouse, "Why would a looker like that go out with a loser like me?"

Women, while waiting in the car as your date gasses up his beater, you look longingly at the distinguished gentleman pumping high-octane fuel into his Jaguar and you ask yourself, "Why can't I ever get a guy like that?"

Deep down, you know you're worthy. "If only they got to know me, they'd recognize my good qualities and fall in love with me."

Yet in the meantime, you keep dating people beneath you. Why? The reasons may run deeper than you think!

"Like what?" you ask. For one, you may be afraid to go for someone better, and you don't want to risk injury to your ego if you're not successful. Two, you might have had a painful breakup with a mate who, at the time, you thought was "out of your league." So now you're gun-shy. Or you may feel you don't have enough money, education, or looks to hobnob with a better class of people. Yet you know you're "too good" for anyone in the pool of potential partners you've been swimming in.

What's happening? The answer is that you've probably recently become more discriminating. It's just like newly slender people who, immediately following a dramatic weight loss, have a "lag factor" before updating their physical self-image. You're probably suffering a lag factor in the league of partner you think you could "get." You're still settling for the same dates who would have satisfied you several years ago—but no longer do.

Or maybe you've tried, but haven't learned, the techniques to capture a better mate. You haven't consciously worked on the necessary qualities to "make the kill." You can lure a street cat to your doorstep with a saucer of milk—but big game won't even glance at it. Likewise, high-quality people are different from the masses, and they are lured by different attributes.

It's Time for an Upgrade

It's now time to update your self-worth and upgrade your skills to capture the partner you used to think was out of your league. As you become more discerning, you realize it is not quantity that counts in life, it's quality. Smart folks don't want lots of clothes, lots of furniture, or lots of relationships. They want a wardrobe of only wonderful outfits, a home filled with only fine furniture, and a life replete with only meaningful relationships.

And in love, our most significant relationship, we want just one really fine quality man or woman with whom we can share a life. We're calling this mate you once thought out of your league a *Princess* or *Prince*.

Practically every young girl, while tucking the covers daintily around herself each night, dreams of the handsome Prince who will someday come riding by on his majestic horse, fall in love with her, and scoop her up, with the two of them then living together happily ever after. Practically every young boy, when he first starts to shave, eyes himself admiringly in the mirror and imagines the Princess of a girl who will swoon over him and fall immediately into his arms gasping, "Take me, I'm yours!"

Well, our dreams haven't changed. But our definition of a Prince or Princess grew up with us. And for each one of us, the connotation of a Royal Catch is different. Perhaps you don't mind if your Princess or Prince is from the wrong side of the tracks— but you want her or him to be extremely kind, sensitive, or intelligent. Or you crave a loving mate of integrity or of culture. Perhaps you want a man or woman with knowledge, wisdom, humor, fidelity, spirituality, or skill. Or maybe it is fame. And, yes, for many, it can be someone with a fortune.

The list goes on, and for everyone it's different. The one unifying factor is that you are ready to start UpDating, which means finding a high-quality person—someone a whole lot better than the frogs you've been croaking with.

Who Is My Prince or Princess?

For almost ten years I have been teaching communication and relationship seminars. Whenever participants bemoaned the fact that they couldn't find anyone "better" to date, I asked them what constitutes "better." Overwhelmingly, they said either "smarter," "better looking," "more interesting," "higher class," "richer," or

> ## RESOLUTION #1
> ## GO FOR SOMEONE "BETTER"
>
> You accept this resolution between your ears. Just as a
> spider can't catch a fly without weaving a web, you
> must weave a good psychological web to catch a
> superior partner. That starts with the deep assurance—
> consciously and subconsciously—that you deserve
> someone better.

"someone with more integrity." Hunters and Huntresses of love,
just like you need a very different type of trap to catch a butter-
fly or a bear, you need very different qualities to catch an honorable partner, a beautiful mate, a rich or high-class paramour, or a
creative companion. Each pursuit demands a particular set of
skills and specific qualities. I'm going to provide you with both.

A Word on UpDating Words

A note on terminology before we continue. Gentlemen, please
don't get paranoid about the frog analogy. True, according to song
and legend, the personified frog is usually of the male gender.
Just like before we got all politically correct and the pronoun *he*
used to denote male or female—our word *frog* denotes both genders of folks you've been DownDating. Frogs are the poor male
or female amphibians you must give your hopping-away papers to.
A frog is the male or female person you used to dig but now know

RESOLUTION #2

MAKE DIFFERENT PLANS FOR DIFFERENT PARTNERS

Just as the spider's web won't bag a bear and flies would soar right through a bear trap, each different type of exceptional partner will require you to use a different type of trapping. One who is gorgeous, one who is high class or rich, one who is honorable, one who is creative—each is lured by different techniques.

you must drown in order to start dating higher up on the human food chain.

Language lesson is over.

1 What's Keeping Me Back?

So Why Do I Keep Dating Frogs?

Fasten your seat belt. This may be a rough ride for some readers. You may not be conscious of it, but the reason you're still going out with second stringers could boil down to a deficiency in the self-esteem department. You may think you have no problem in that area. But unless you're dating your equals or better, you have a big problem. Why?

Because we do not go after who we want. We only go after who we think we deserve!

"Not me," some of you might say. "I always go after what I want." Perhaps you do. But what you may not know is, unless you have true subconscious unwavering belief in yourself, you're sure to botch it up.

Women, you could aim your arrow at the nicest and best-looking man in your church, community, or company. You might even make a play for him. But unfortunately, unless you are subconsciously and profoundly confident you deserve such a fine partner, you'll muck it up in minuscule ways. You'll try to relax and swing your hips comfortably as you pass him—but your tension will make it look like you need hip replacement. You may bat your eyelashes seductively—but your nervousness makes it come across as an ocular astigmatism. Without confidence, you cannot carry any ploy off with the necessary panache.

Gentlemen, you might even ask the accomplished angel-faced woman at work for the pleasure of her company at dinner. But unless you subconsciously feel she'd be the lucky one to get you, your insecurity will stick out like a dirty shirttail and she'll turn you down. After all, if you don't think you're terrific, she won't either.

Bugs and Beasts Are Smarter When Choosing a Mate

When choosing "the one," a female penguin knows better than to fall for the first nerd who waddles up and honks. She holds out for the fittest suitor available, which, in Antarctica, means one tubby enough to sit for weeks on her newly hatched eggs without starving to death. Female scorpion flies are also fussy. They scorn unsymmetrical manbugs and only flirt with invertebrate lovers who have well-matched wings. Ladybugs opt for males who are most masterful at killing prey and bringing home the bacon.

So, if penguins and flies don't settle, why should you? The reasons are many—and often bizarre. Frequently, your settling for life in the froggery has to do with your own loneliness or need for support. Maybe it's just because you want easy sex. Or perhaps you enjoy having a slave who, although he or she is not up to your standards, will do anything for you.

Many people get into a relationship they're all excited about at first. Perhaps it's happened to you. You meet someone. He or she is stimulating and fun to be with. So you start thinking about a long-term relationship.

Then little by little you begin discovering your partner's nasty little habits. He or she tells a lie, cheats, or passes gas in public. The disappointments pile up on you one by one, and you begin to realize this is not the ideal mate you once hoped he or she would be. Perhaps you keep telling yourself things will change and your partner will become Mr. or Ms. Right. But deep down you know you're kidding yourself. Time passes and you do nothing about it.

Sometimes, when you're feeling low, you tell yourself you won't find anyone better. Then when it hits you that this person doesn't live up to your standards, you kick yourself, knowing you should make the move. But you don't. Why? Because although on a conscious level you feel worthy of a wondrously fulfilling relationship with a world-class partner, on a subconscious level you're telling yourself a very different story.

See if you recognize any of these hidden hang-ups in yourself.

Hang-Up #1: Fear of Failure

This is a biggie in every aspect of life. Instead of concentrating on all the joy and happiness you will gain in your new life with

TECHNIQUE #1
RENOUNCE REBOUND REACTIONS

If the Prince doesn't ask you out, or if the Princess turns you down, do not make an immediate date with a frog just to reaffirm your desirability. Lick your wounds and go hunt up another someone worthy of your love.

a Prince(ess), you focus on what you'll lose if you're not successful. Suppose you make a pass or flirt with a Royal Potential Mate, and he or she ignores you. Ouch, that hurts. The only type of mate you are sure of success with is—you guessed it—another frog. So there you go again, diving back into the frog pond for a date.

Hang-Up #2: Staying with the Familiar

You may be so accustomed to life in the frog pond that it's difficult to jump out. Frogs are familiar. Frogs are routine. Frogs are comfortable. Frogs are a habit—a bad habit.

I know routine is hard to break, but the only way to do it is to go cold turkey. Say, "No!" to the next frog who says, "Let's go out together."

TECHNIQUE #2
GO COLD TURKEY ON FROGS

Constantly dating people beneath you is a bad habit like smoking, drinking, compulsive eating, or shopping 'til you drop. It feels good at the moment, but it hurts big-time in the long run. One cigarette, one drink, one chocolate binge, one shopping spree—and you've failed. Likewise, one more date with a frog and you've failed.

Hang-Up #3: Being Emotionally Needy

You hunger for love—and frogs feed your voracious appetite. They adore you. And why not? They're getting a good deal in the relationship. You may be smarter, richer, more attractive, a better person, and a whole lot cooler than they are. They'd be nuts not to want you.

Get rid of that excess baggage of being "emotionally needy" and desperately needing love. Reaffirm your worth by reviewing all the assets you bring to a relationship. Let a little self-love replace the unhealthy craving for love from just anybody.

TECHNIQUE #3
NIX EMOTIONAL NEEDINESS

When you feel lonely and crave love or sex, recognize that you could just be suffering from a bout of emotional neediness. Now's the time to make a list of your good qualities and reasons why a quality partner would be lucky to get you. This will dissipate the desire for "one more time" with any current dates.

Hang-Up #4: Feeling Life and Love Are Predestined

Do you feel it's out of your hands and that someday your Prince(ess) will come? Do you just sit in front of the television with your current frog and wait?

Now we're dealing with a real problem. I am not here to argue with your spiritual or religious convictions. I respect and hold many such beliefs myself. But let me tell you a story I heard from the eminent psychologist David Lieberman that I think will make the point.[1]

A terrible hurricane swept through a small town and the flooding was awful. The water rose higher and higher until only the treetops and the roofs of a few houses were visible. It was as if an ocean had emptied into the streets.

A man in a rowboat came up alongside a woman who was clutching the cross on top of a church a few feet above the rising water. "Let's go, Ma'am," the man in the boat said.

But the woman refused to step into the boat. "Oh, no," she said. "God would not let me die." So the boatman rowed off in the storm to save someone else clutching a treetop.

A little while later, a second boatman came by offering to take her to safety. "Oh, no," she repeated, clutching the cross tighter. "God would not let me die." And off this boatman went, battling the increasingly high waves to save other stranded folks.

The torrential storm didn't let up, and the water soared higher and higher. It was now menacingly swirling around the woman's knees. A helicopter flying overhead swooped down and dropped a ladder to take her to safety. "Oh, no," she shouted up to the pilot. "God would not let me die." So off flew the helicopter.

The water rose higher, the hurricane raged stronger, and finally a fierce gust of wind swept the woman off the church steeple. And she drowned.

When she passed through heaven's gate, God appeared in front of her.

"How could you let me die?" she screamed. "I put my faith in you."

God answered, "I tried to save you, my child. I sent you two boats and a helicopter. You let yourself die."

Technique #4
Dump the Destiny Bit

Need I say more? Even if you think you are destined to find a Princess or Prince, get off your tush and search.

What If Some Frogs Still Turn Me On?

Maybe some of the frogs you've been dating aren't nerds. But they are other kinds of undesirable amphibians. Some of them might be sexy or fascinating or mysterious. Even rich or good looking or clever. But you know many of these dates are not "good people," not the right ones for you.

If this is the case, don't feel guilty. You are not alone. The professional journal *Violence and Victims* published a study exploring why women are attracted to the "bad boys."[2] Men, too, find themselves getting tangled up in costly relationships.

Why the lure of the rogue or rogue-ette? Often it's because we feel our life lacks drama. We remember the discovery, the excitement, the excruciating pain and intense pleasure of always being on the brink of disaster with our first loves. Later in life, you may have developed the "Ho-hum, I've been there and done that" feeling about lovers. Then you need a higher and higher threshold of what it takes to get the old juices flowing again. When you are confused or even abused by a current partner, it recaptures the melodramatic moments of your first loves. You can get high on the thrill and, if you're not careful, become a love junkie for these sexy scoundrels.

There's another reason these sexy rats and rat-ettes turn us on. Most of them are, to all outward appearances, completely confident. They look and sound like they know what they want. And they push others around to get it. When so many other people suffer from insecurity, their arrogance can be a big turn-on.

Technique #5
Purge Your Pool of Sexy Frogs, Too

If you are currently dating anyone not worthy of you, get rid of him or her immediately. Warning: staying with a bad boy or bad girl may be harmful to your morals, thereby disqualifying you for your eventual Prince or Princess. Even if the frog is sexy, tough, and exciting, get out of the relationship while the getting is good.

But just as we grew up and realized a diet of Oreo cookies and hot fudge sundaes was not good for us, we begin to realize that many attractive sexy people are really frogs in foxy-looking clothes. It's time to let go.

Don't regret the past. Dating frogs was fine for a while. You probably learned a lot from them. And, in turn, you did your philanthropic bit for the frogs of the world by giving them not only your time and maybe your money but also your heart. But at last, you've gained the wisdom that they're not worthy of you. And it's time to move on.

Each of us has reasons and rationales for having populated our life with frogs. No matter how much we think if we kiss them, they'll turn into a Prince or a Princess, somehow they never do. Our dud dates keep letting us down and down and down until we're drowning in their pond.

Time to Play for Keeps

I liken the search for a wonderful mate to listening to the car radio. When we were young, we dug all kinds of music. We went racing down the highway of life, radio at full blast. We'd groove on scan—hear a few seconds of acid rock, a few seconds of rap, some C&W, and a few seconds of traffic and weather together.

Then as we got older, things started to change. We turned down the volume and found another sound track for life. Now our radio was on seek. We'd seek for a while until we found a station we liked. We'd listen for a while until it got repetitive, and then we'd move on.

Finally, as adults, most of us want a high-quality station we really like so we can set our button for keeps.

It's the same with love. Most of us *scanned* relationships. Maybe we dated someone funny for a while. When we tired of cheap laughs, we'd try somebody else. Perhaps we then went for someone "deep." But we soon wearied of pondering the universe and our navels. Then we'd dig someone who made the universe shake for us—sexually. But we got disillusioned when there was nothing to talk about "afterward."

A few years later, we decided to *seek*. We searched until we found someone we liked. We'd go steady or even live with that person. But when we found ourselves wanting to drown out everything our partner said, we'd ram our thumb into the button and seek some more.

So you can see that in love, too, there is a time to scan and a time to seek—but then there comes a time to *set your life for keeps*. Picking up this book means you are probably at this stage.

Technique #6
Set Your Dial for Keeps

You've heard kids singing "Finders Keepers," right? No different here. You won't be with the person you want to be with "for keeps" unless you first find him or her. Promise yourself you'll read all forty-nine proven techniques in *UpDating!* and put them into practice. It's hard work but the rewards are priceless. You'll win a lifetime with the Prince or Princess who was once just a dream.

You want to set your life with the one high-quality man or woman with whom you can make beautiful music forever.

And that's just what I'm going to help you do.

All Proven Fact, No Pulp Fiction

Every time I walk into a bookstore or look at a magazine rack, I am thunderstruck by the number of doctors, psychologists, writers, and other "experts" who counsel on love. Most of what I read is based on the author's bird's-eye view of romance. There are, of course, some outstanding exceptions, but even many of those are not based on concrete studies.

In the twenty-first century, we have the results of hundreds of studies of what actually works in love and what doesn't. I covered the proven answers to many questions about love in my earlier book *How to Make Anyone Fall in Love with You* (Contemporary Books, 1996), which should serve as prerequisite reading to *UpDating!*

We now know whether "love at first sight" is a myth or a reality. We know why we're attracted to one person and not another— even if the "another" is better looking, smarter, richer, and all the etceteras. We know the precise choreography of moves necessary to execute a successful pickup. We know what the most love-inducing first date is. We know whether playing hard to get works. We even know whether men like lipstick on a woman and whether women prefer men in glasses. All this and the results of many other love studies were covered in *How to Make Anyone Fall in Love with You*.

There was a reason the first book said "Anyone." It's because many of us were in the scanning or seeking mode then. It was fun to use the techniques I wrote about on a variety of people and watch them *all* flip over us. But now it's time to broaden our horizons, narrow our choices, upgrade our love life, and set our button for keeps.

Researchers Write in a Code Called *Impossible to Read*

I find it interesting that most of the studies seriously exploring this thing called *love* are written in an almost foreign language. For instance, when the researchers want to say, "How a man and woman who live together get along," they compose confounding phrases like *dyadic function of heterosexual cohabiters*. Instead of simply saying two people "want to live near each other," the sociologists come up with *intentional propinquity*. When they want to express "they don't think alike," they choose the bewildering *cognitive dissonance*. The words may impress editors of sociological journals, but they leave the rest of us scratching our heads.

Researchers also go ballistic naming their studies. Would you be tempted to pick up a book called *An Ecological Determinant of Differential Amounts of Sociometric Choices*? No wonder much of the serious research that has given us the bottom line on love remains buried on back shelves of library archives.

Perhaps it's perverse, but knowing what gold is entombed within the studies, I actually enjoyed deciphering them. With a pile of medical and sociological dictionaries on the library table, I blew away the dust and plowed through hundreds of them. Every time I discovered a gem, I plucked it out with tweezers, held it up to the test of truth, and wove it into a technique to help you achieve your more lofty love goals.

You'll find this book is very different from others in another way. Bookstore shelves are filled with guides to winning admirers, lovers, or a spouse. Some few have even concentrated on getting a rich husband or wife. But none, to date, has centered on finding one truly high-quality mate. Much of the advice you'll read elsewhere is generic, intended to work on practically anyone of the opposite sex. Unfortunately, when it comes to a Princess or Prince, most of the old tricks don't work.

Huntresses of love, suppose for the moment your definition of a Prince is a man who is extremely wealthy *and* cultured. Well, the advice of winking and wiggling seductively could actually turn him off. Oh, it may get you a ride in his Mercedes (most likely in the backseat behind some high bushes) but not a ring on your finger.

Hunters of love, suppose your definition of a quality mate is a woman who is extremely beautiful and spiritual. Your flashing a big fat wallet may make her glance your way but not give you her heart. Many methods employed to entice the majority of men or women are fruitless when your quarry is a Princess or Prince.

TECHNIQUE #7
CHUCK CHEAP TRICKS

Many methods you may have used to turn on the "dude" sitting in the bar guzzling beer, or the "chick" whose skirt is too tight and morals too loose, won't work on a quality mate. High-caliber people love sex, of course, but the come-on or lines are more subtle. We'll learn some of the elusive lures. Don't worry—they read between the lines.

So What's the Secret?

What is the magic potion to make a quality man or woman fall in love with you? The formula is quite simple, actually—and yet complex.

1. You must swear off DownDating all unworthy candidates. No exceptions!
2. Then you must have a deep conversation with yourself and decide what you consider to be the perfect potential mate.
3. The next task is to learn all about that particular type of person—your desired mate's tastes, beliefs, values, and goals, as well as what he or she holds dear.

Technique #8
Give Yourself a Personal Checkup

As you read *UpDating!*, perform a checklist on yourself and possibly make some changes in either your surface or substantial qualities. I will guide you in both self-revelations and, if necessary, renovations. I'll show you how to emulate your desired mate's superficial qualities to get his or her attention.

Then we'll work on your becoming more like them at a deeper level. When you, too, become a true Princess or Prince, you have the "currency" to buy a Royal heart and keep his or her love and respect forever.

4. Now for the hard part. You must stare at yourself in the mirror like you've never seen your face before. Do you look and sound like the type of man or woman you want? Do you fit in with his or her elevated crowd? Then gaze more deeply into the looking glass of your life to see if you've "got the goods" to make your desired mate consider you a worthy lifelong partner.

There are two parts to your self-searching and transformation—two major categories of qualities you must excel in to capture a world-class partner. There is the *surface* and there is the *substantial.* The surface (some would say "superficial") consists of how you wear your hair, how you dress, what words you use, and in some cases, knowing how to eat an artichoke or knowing not to drink from your finger bowl. The substantial runs deeper. Here you explore qualities like your integrity, your self-knowledge, your spirituality, your confidence, your thought processes, and how loving you are.

The Horse-Trading Principle of Love

Why have I used such a crass word like *currency*? Actually, it's because of the overwhelming response to a few paragraphs I wrote in *How to Make Anyone Fall in Love with You* which likened love to bartering. Here are the paragraphs that kindled the firestorm of letters and E-mails asking for more:

> During a heated argument, a man I once loved snarled at me, "Everybody's got a value on the open market, baby." I was appalled. How crass! How could he see people as commodities, especially somebody he said he loved? What a repulsive way to look at relationships!

To me, love was beautiful. Love was pure. It was the source of the most intense human pleasure known to mankind and had no parallel in human experience. To me, love was sharing, trusting, total giving of self. The words of Robert Burns had reverberated in my heart since childhood: "Love, O lyric Love, half angel and half bird. And all a wonder and a wild desire." To hear my lover liken his loved one's qualities to pork bellies or soybeans on the commodities market was too much. I stormed out of the room. And, soon thereafter, out of the relationship.

Now, many years later, older and, some few could argue, wiser, I wonder, "Was he right?" Not in his manner of presentation, certainly. But in his facts? It surprises no one to hear, "Everyone wants to get the best deal possible in life." Nor are they shocked when they learn about the law of supply and demand in business. People don't even flinch when sales gurus preach that, in all human interaction, the big question is WIIFM—what's in it for me?

Why do we recoil when researchers tell us the same natural laws apply to love?

Recently, the scientific community, not content with theories of love proposed by Sigmund Freud (sublimated sexuality) or Theodore Reik (filling a void in oneself), set out to get the real skinny on love. Conducting numerous surveys and laboratory experiments, scientists peeled back a deeper layer of the human psyche. Did they uncover some ugly facts? Did they confront a monster? Some might say, "Yes." Others would laugh it off and say, "Of course not."

Whether you see their findings as the abominable snowman or the archangel of truth, the result is quite simply this: Studies do indeed support the thesis that everything and everybody has a quantifiable value on the open market. And everybody wants to get the best deal possible in love as well as in life. Researchers christened their findings the *equity* (or *exchange*) *theory of love*. It's sort of like the old *horse-trading principle*.

The equity theory of love is based on the same sound business principles of barter and open market value. Everything has a value. Everything has a price. As with that of a product, a person's value can be subjective. Generally, the world agrees on what's a good catch and what's a shoddy one.

In the world of horse trading, there are *top-grade champions* or *nags* (horses ready for the glue factory). At a horse auction, buyers look for qualities they describe as *pretty movers*, *good disposition*, *no bad vices*, and even *flashy*. Are humans really so different?

All these horse qualities affect the sales price. If you are trading a registered horse for one without pedigree papers, he better have some of the other superior qualities to make it a fair barter.

Studies show that the more qualities you bring to the bargaining table, the better you will do in love. The more your assets even out, the more apt you are to make someone fall in love with you. Equity theorists tell us the more equitable a romantic relationship is, the more likely it is to progress to marriage.[3]

So you might ask, "Does that mean, if I want a very rich partner, do I need to become a billionaire?" Or, "If I want a very beautiful person, do I need to have plastic surgery or leg implants to make me six inches taller?" Of course not. Because, as love researchers tell us, you don't need to have the *same* assets. Your and your intended partner's assets simply need to even out. The classic example is the drop-dead gorgeous woman you see on the arm of an old curmudgeon. What do you think? Admit it— *money*! If she's a "10" in looks, he's probably a "10" in the lucre department.

Another example might be the brilliant and handsome stock-broker who marries an ordinary-looking woman. But when you get to know her better, you discover she is deeply spiritual. Yet

Technique #9
Realize That Love Is a Tough Business

Believe it when people tell you love is exhilarating, love is exciting, love is beautiful. But don't let them kid you that love is blind. Finding a permanent partner is one of the most carefully considered and calculated risks you will take in life. Even the loftiest folks look at long-term love like a business deal. Acquiring a lifelong partner is too important a "purchase" to take a chance on getting a lemon. Don't be naive. Realize that love is one tough business deal.

another example might be the highly moral minister of the local parish who chooses to marry a less ethical woman. Most likely, it would soon become evident that she has other "assets," perhaps an effervescent personality and outstanding social graces, which help him keep the parish together. Researchers tell us that partners in the happiest and most secure relationships don't necessarily excel in the *same* qualities, but they bring equal assets to the table.

It's just like weighing the value of a purchase. Even the nicest people instinctively calculate their potential partner's "comparable worth." They examine the "hidden costs." They project the "maintenance-free." They factor in the "assumed depreciation." Overall, they are subconsciously calculating the "cost-benefit ratio" of the relationship.

And, of course, they want to make darn sure they don't suffer "buyer's remorse." One of the safest ways to do this is to stick with what they know. Similarity is safe for everyone, even for Royals.

You Gotta Be One to Get One

As I told you, when I asked participants in my relationship seminars what type of mate they most wanted, I heard a cacophony of answers like "more intelligent," "better looking," "more sensitive" "honest," "a good person," or someone with more "money," "creativity," "education," or "integrity." But the word I heard most often was "class."

After discussing it for a while, everyone usually agrees the word *class* symbolizes all of the above. Why? Because many of the aforementioned enviable qualities often come as a package. Someone with class often is intelligent, honest, educated, rich, creative, and even good looking.

Why is that? Someone with money, especially old-family money, has the time to explore "the finer things in life" and

develop "classier" tastes. They have the leisure, the encourage-
ment, and the freedom to be more creative.

Integrity often accompanies class because there's no monetary
reason to not act with integrity. Someone truly intelligent knows
you get along a lot better in life if you are honorable and have
good taste. When you're rich, you can also afford the best
education.

So how does "good looking" factor into this? When you're
rich, you can buy the most flattering clothes, go to spas, and even
pay a cosmetic surgeon to fix up any dirty tricks Mother Nature
played on you.

There are, of course, many exceptions to this bundling-of-
qualities rule. Someone who is flat broke and with very little
integrity could be as classy as Old English typeface. A refined individual, cultured enough to introduce to the queen, could be dirt
poor. A multimillionaire could pick his nose at a state dinner. A
deeply honorable or wise individual could have as much class as
an alley cat. And any of the above could be as beautiful as a
Greek god or goddess or as ugly as a dead toad. But not usually.
The qualities often go together.

Birds of a Royal Feather

Did you ever notice how the rich *usually* marry the rich, the beautiful *usually* marry the beautiful, and the famous *usually* marry the
famous? Coupling is far more apt to happen when each partner
has an abundance of the same qualities. It is usual and very common to see rich marrying rich, beautiful marrying beautiful, and
famous marrying famous. But people with the more substantial
qualities—like good character and intelligence—almost *always*
marry people with equally substantial qualities. High-quality peo-

ple don't want to spend a lifetime with someone who is dishonest or unprincipled.

Why are there more exceptions to the rich, the famous, or the beautiful marrying someone with the same assets? Because a rich person who has enough money for two is not negatively affected by someone with a small bank account. A good-looking person can be impressed with another's qualifications even if he or she is not a "looker." And a famous person can enjoy being in the limelight and having a less-renowned spouse.

But it is rare indeed if a highly principled man or woman can love someone whose way of looking at life is not equally honorable and ethical. So the bottom line is, if you want to make someone with high standards fall in love with you, you, too, must become equally principled and honorable.

"Got it," one of my students said. "If I want a terrific mate, the answer is just going out and becoming equally terrific—either in money, looks, brains, culture, prestige, character, or any of the above."

Not so fast! Unfortunately, that's not the whole answer. You must also grasp the components of attraction and what the studies have proven works and doesn't work. We must never forget, even in the top echelon of society, that sex counts! Princes and Princesses enjoy doing much the same things in bed that the rest of us do. But getting one into our bed requires a special set of skills.

Similarity Runs Even Deeper

In addition to factors like looks, money, and intelligence, people are attracted to those who are similar in what the researchers call *social characteristics*. Social characteristics cover such things as your tendency to be a recluse or a party animal, how many friends and relationships you've had, how your folks got along, and even how you now feel about your dad.

There are some things you can change, some you can't, and others you wouldn't want to. We'll dig deeper into similarities later and discuss what qualities you must radiate in order to lure an incredible mate. But just for starters, let me quote a landmark study that explored the most common ways in which married or longtime partners were alike. According to the *American Journal of Sociology*, similarity was found with respect to the following:

- Family background, including place lived in childhood, educational level, nativity income, and social status of parents
- Religious affiliation
- Types of family relationships, including happiness of parents' marriage, attitude toward the father when a child, and sex of siblings
- Social participation, including the tendency to be a lone wolf rather than socially gregarious, leisure time preference ("stay at home" versus "on the go"), drinking habits, smoking habits, number of friends of the same sex or opposite sex
- Courtship behavior (such as previously being engaged and the number of people dated steadily) and attitude toward marriage

Now obviously, you can't change such things as how happy your parents' marriage was, the number of brothers and sisters you have, or the number of people you've had relationships with. Nor, probably, would you want to change your religious affiliation. But there are some things you can change to rate a better mate. You can develop similar attitudes in life, which is all important. These are aspects like your perspective on money, friends, leisure-time activities, and marriage.

You already have a head start in all this. By picking up *UpDating!*, you've demonstrated one admirable quality: your desire to grow in the areas that have proven to be significant to getting a superior partner.

That's a lot of work, isn't it? Yes, it is. But I'm sure someone in your life has spouted the old verity "You get what you pay for." However, we're not talking money here. Close your wallet but open your mind. In this case, you are paying with your valuable time and your dedication to get the man or woman you once thought out of your league.

TECHNIQUE #10
ACT ROYAL, 'ROUND THE CLOCK

Go for it! Make the qualities you gain to capture your superior mate part of your life, not just when you're "hunting." You'll respect yourself more—and so will everyone else. As you become the man or woman who attracts a high-quality person, you, too, become a high-quality person. And that's a very cool state!

The Big Bonus

By now, no doubt, you've guessed what the added benefit is to reading *UpDating!* During the process of learning what it takes to win a better mate, you'll probably get to know yourself in a different way than you ever thought possible. If you decide instead of just using the techniques to win a superior partner, you want to make them part of your life (as I deeply hope you will), you will become a much better person. Make the changes permanent. Really become the person you know he or she could fall and stay in love with forever. As you emit the qualities that attract a first-rate mate, you may begin to like the new you—and so will everyone else!

You Won't Find Your Prince or Princess Until You Go Cold Turkey on Frogs

Paving the Path for a Better Mate

Good. You've decided you're ready for the course in Capturing a Better Partner. But wait—before you're admitted to the Advanced School of Love you must take a prerequisite. What is it? I learned it from a little tyke with a six year old's penetrating wisdom.

I was once visiting a girlfriend in New York. We had just finished a late dinner and her little son decided to escape from his bedroom and join the conversation. As his mother started to pick up the dishes, she winked at me and said to him, "Arnold, you can stay here, but you must entertain Auntie Leil while I tidy up the kitchen." He didn't seem too thrilled with the prospect. But, I guess, figuring I was a relative (wrongly, because I was one of those aunts by assimilation), he felt obligated.

I asked him the conventional question you ask a kid when you don't know what else to talk about. "So, Arnold, what do you want to be when you grow up?"

"An architect," he answered almost too quickly. He exuded a pride and certitude beyond his years. Suspecting that he had rehearsed that line just to impress grown-ups, I said, "Oh, and what type of buildings do you want to build?"

"Big ones," he replied smugly, stretching his arms out wide, pushing out his tiny chest, and arrogantly pulling himself up to his full one yard and one inch of height.

I decided to challenge the pompous little tadpole. I asked, "Really? And what's the first thing you do when you build a big building?"

He stared at me incredulously. "Anybody knows the answer to that one. You tear down the old one." I must admit, I was impressed. Little Arnold was absolutely right, at least for New York City, where he lived.

The analogy to love is perfect. That's precisely what we must do when we want to start UpDating. You've got to ring out the old to bring in the new. Some of the old behavior that worked with the frogs you've been hanging with has got to go.

Behavior, for the most part, is governed by habit. And now it's time to start developing better habits—from your clothes to your creed in life. You must do this to earn the prize, the Prince or Princess you deserve.

How Do I Start?

First step: do not continue hopping from pad to pad in the frog pond. Understand that you are after bigger-league game now. Give all frogs their hopping papers—*immediately*!

Why do you need to swear off all frogs before you find your Prince or Princess? Why not wait until you find your superb partner? Because there are universal natural laws in life and in love. This one is as basic as air and water. When air or water is sucked away from a space, more flows into it.

So it is in love. When you take away any current main squeeze, you've psychologically made room for another. It's only when you're alone that you start seeking a replacement in earnest.

You might be tempted to say, "Oh, I'll just keep seeing a few frogs until my dream partner comes along." Sorry, it doesn't work that way. The thousands of little thought processes and actions you take when you're mentally or physically "with" someone keep you from finding another.

Think about it. You and your ho-hum date are sitting in a restaurant. He or she is happily chatting away. You stifle a yawn and your sleepy eyes sweep the room. Suddenly, blam! You spot your potential partner—sitting alone! You smile. Desirable stranger smiles back.

Alas, that's the end of it. Because you're with Froggie, your dream partner looks away—probably at the other attractive stranger of the opposite sex dining alone at the quiet little table in the corner. Rats! You know if old Froggie hadn't been sitting across from you, you'd have a good chance at starting your UpDating campaign right then and there.

Wait, it gets worse. It's not just when you're with someone that your chance of finding a better catch is almost nil. The knowledge that you're not going to be alone on Saturday night—ol' faithful will be there—keeps you from scheming to meet someone new.

So what if you're dateless for a month or two? You'll learn to get comfortable going out alone—especially to places where exceptional people hang out. I'll show you later, due to the proven *exposure theory*, how this astronomically increases your chances of capturing a first-class mate.

Technique #11

Resolve to Rid Yourself of All Unsuitable Partners

This is an important psychological step. Realize that until all frogs are history, you'll have no future with a Prince or Princess. You must give all current amphibians their hopping papers before you even begin the royal hunt.

Doing the Dirty Deed

If there is one regular current frog in your life, there are many ways to do the dreaded deed of exterminating him or her. It is much simpler if your relationship is new and you've gone from frog attraction to frog revulsion in a matter of weeks. Gentlemen, in this case, you simply stop calling her. Women, you simply tell the toad you're seeing someone else.

However, when the frog has been in your pond for months or more, it becomes increasingly complex. In that case, you must find a kinder and gentler way, and yet one that is honest and final, to deal with your longtime frog. If you don't, you are in dire danger of living in the swamp forever.

Recently, I was giving a speech in Washington, D.C., my old hometown. My hotel room phone rang, and a woman with a trace of a Portuguese accent said, "Leilie, this is a voice from the past." I immediately recognized it. She was a wonderful friend from school days. Isabel had been a fabulously talented girl who introduced the whole school to fado music. It was her passion. On Saturday nights, she and any other of us girls who didn't have a date would sit around while Isabel entertained us by strumming the guitar and singing fado songs. The haunting sound of her voice often brought me to tears. Her voice embodied the soulful, almost sad, mourning passion that is the essence of fado.

To top it off, Isabel had an enviable figure and long lustrous black hair. I would have hated her if I hadn't liked her so much. We called her "the dark-haired diva," and we all believed in our hearts she was going to be the Judy Garland of fado.

Isabel had a second passion in her life. It was a man who fit her definition of a Prince precisely. Her Prince was named Joam. He was an up-and-coming fado singer whom she had met when he was on tour in the United States.

Joam was also infatuated with Isabel. He was constantly on tour, however, and theirs was a long-distance relationship. Joam wrote to Isabel every few weeks and called her from time to time. But this wasn't enough for her. She thought about Joam around the clock, and I could tell, whenever she was singing her sad songs, she was thinking about him. The yearning chants were coming from her heart. Yet because Isabel came from a very strict background, she didn't make any aggressive moves to capture her Prince. She felt the man should always be the aggressor. So she simply waited for his letters and his calls.

There was another man in Isabel's life, a loyal and devoted fellow named Fernandez. Fernandez adored Isabel. He wanted to be with her wherever she went. He took her shopping. He chauffeured her wherever she wanted to go. He even accompanied her to her singing coach each week. And he'd always wait in the car, like the faithful frog he was, to drive her home.

Unfortunately, Fernandez was not very cultured, rich, or talented. His biggest talent seemed to be keeping track of Isabel's every move. Isabel told me time and time again she was going to break off with him. But she waffled, she vacillated, and she made constant excuses for keeping him around. I guess she found it difficult to think of life without a manservant. She'd continually ask me what I thought of Fernandez, and I was apprehensive about giving her my honest opinion.

Finally, at our graduation ceremony, Isabel announced her resolution. She was definitely going to break the bad news to Fernandez the following week.

That's when I lost touch with Isabel. Life took us our separate ways. I thought about her often and half expected to see her name on a marquee somewhere announcing the diva of fado in concert. Unfortunately, that phone call in Washington was the next time I heard her voice.

We met for dinner that night, and instead of the anticipated joy, I felt sad when I saw her. There was no longer the electric passion in Isabel's eyes. Her body was no longer tight, and she was dressed more like a housewife than a fado diva. I could almost guess, but I couldn't resist asking about her music, her beloved Joam, and all the other things that had at one time made her life so passionate.

With a melancholy voice she told me that she had become upset with Joam because he didn't visit or call more often. And since Fernandez was so faithful, she got used to having him around. She finally married him and . . .

Isabel's voice trailed off. I could tell if she'd continued, she would have said, "and it was the biggest mistake of my life." Apparently, Fernandez was no longer putting his best foot forward. He had become less attentive and, as she said, "very boring."

"And Joam?" I asked. Now her voice took on an almost tragic tone. When she'd told Joam she was going to be married, he never contacted her again. After all, Joam was a man of honor.

Then the poignant part. She told me she had read in the newspaper a few years ago that he was coming to Washington on tour. Isabel, of course, went to his concert. After his performance, she gathered up the courage to go backstage to talk with him. When Joam saw her, she said more passion came into his eyes than she'd seen onstage that night. With difficult-to-maintain restraint, he told her how much he'd loved her and that he'd always intended to make her his wife. He'd envisioned them touring and perhaps even singing together. He told her how devastated he had been when she'd told him of her upcoming nuptials.

Time had passed, and Joam eventually married a girl from Lisbon who had been one of his faithful fans for years. The only joy Isabel saw in Joam's face that evening was when he pulled out a photo of his two beautiful children. She then showed him a photo of her daughter. Isabel told me that they looked at each other and, for a brief moment, she knew they had the same thought: "These beautiful children should have been ours."

Joam had married his frogette, and Isabel had married her frog. And, I thought sadly, "they lived unhappily ever after." We all three knew their lives were nothing compared to what they could have been. And it all would have been different if Isabel had had the courage to break up with her frog and concentrate on "capturing" her Prince. Or if Joam had been more aggressive in going after his Princess.

Don't let this happen to you. Immediately swear off spending time with any unworthy mates!

The Ditching Dilemma

Remember we spoke about the horse-trading principle of love? It holds true. However, in love, unlike in business, we need to be a bit more sensitive. For example, it is perfectly acceptable for a customer to tell one vendor he's going to buy another's product or service because it's better. But what would you think of lovers who told their current partners, "I'm not going to go out with you anymore because this other person is more interesting, better looking,

Technique #12

PURGE ANY FROGS IN A PRINCELY FASHION

Never be tacky in the way you free yourself of a frog.
Handle it like a Prince or Princess would. The story of
your disentanglement from previous relationships is
bound to come out with your future high quality mate.
And he or she will respect you much more if you did
the dirty deed with class.

richer, or sexier?" Not a cool move. You must be more compassionate. So let's explore how you can do the dreaded deed of getting all unworthy contenders out of your life so you can pave the path for a superior partner.

Women, You Must Ditch or Drown

Males and females have vastly different ways of coming upon the realization that they must expel all frogs from their pond.

First, here's how most women deal with the dilemma (myself included, but I'm trying to reform). We start by drowning ourselves in analyzing the situation to death. Like Isabel, we waffle, we vacillate, and we make constant excuses for the men we're dating. We bore our friends to death asking what they think of them. We even canvass virtual strangers!

I once vacationed at a resort with a then-beloved frog named Fred, and I actually asked the proprietress of the hotel what she thought of him. In fact, I turned every poor soul who ever came within a ten-foot radius of the two of us together into a confused and unwilling consultant.

Many women on the verge of breakup become first-time clients of psychics, channelers, astrologists, or tarot card and palm readers, desperately seeking the answer. Breaking up—should I or shouldn't I? It's like picking the petals off a daisy, except this time we're asking, "Do *I* love him? Do *I* love him not?"

SOMETIMES WE DELUDE OURSELVES THAT OUR FROG IS A PRINCE

When faced with having to exterminate a lover, we deceive ourselves. We think that if we keep kissing frogs, one of them will eventually turn into a Prince. To justify not taking the separation step, we torture ourselves thinking of all the good things about the relationship—especially when we're feeling insecure.

In fact, when you are feeling insecure, that is the time when you are most in danger of not doing the dirty ditching deed. Lack of self-esteem can keep you hooked on DownDating long after you should have upgraded your love life. A four-part study called "The Effect of Self Esteem on Romantic Liking" precisely proved the point.[4]

Part One. Researchers arranged for a group of single women to individually "accidentally" run into a very good-looking man in the hall on the way to an experiment. The man (unbeknownst to the women) was part of the experiment, and the encounter was made to look like a chance meeting.

The researchers had directed the desirable man to then show increasing interest in the woman. After the two of them had chatted for a while, he was to ask her for a dinner-and-show date in San Francisco the following week.

Part Two. Supposedly unrelated, but soon after she made the date, the researchers asked each woman to come to a different room, where she was given a Rorschach ink blot test. When she finished, the researchers handed the evaluation results to the woman.

The poor women had no idea the results were fraudulent. By design, researchers had given half the women false low evaluations. These women received a report card filled with distressing descriptions of themselves supposedly revealed by the ink blot test. They read words like "immature," "weak personality," "antisocial motives," "unoriginal," and "not flexible." (That must have made their day!)

The other half of the women, the control group, received just the opposite. The report from the Rorschach ink blot test stressed their wonderful "sensitivity to peers," "personal integrity," "originality," and "freedom of outlook."

By the way, the fact that people will accept false personality descriptions as accurate had been established previously in a study that researchers called, in big words, *defensive projection.*[5] Accepting what others say about them is especially true of women. Fortune-tellers rely on this heavily. Their crystal ball often "tells" them what the self-credentialed soothsayers pick up from the insecurity or conceit they observe in their clients' demeanor.

Part Three. Back to the deceived women. After sharing the results from the ink blot test, the researchers asked the subjects to meet with a group of peers. The women were directed to have a group conversation, which the researchers interrupted three times. During each recess, every participant was asked to fill out a secret evaluation of the others in the group.

Once again, all the subjects received false "report cards" about how much the other participants liked them. The women who had received the negative Rorschach evaluations were now falsely informed that their colleagues didn't like them. Conversely, participants who had received positive Rorschach reports were told that their peers had positive things to say about them.

Part Four. Finally, the examiners asked each woman how she felt about the man she had previously met in the hall.

Here are the surprising results: the women who had received negative evaluations overwhelmingly liked the guy who had asked them for a date—much more so than the women who were feeling pretty good about themselves. The women's emotions toward the man were greatly affected by their deflated or inflated self-image inspired by the report card. In the researchers' words:

> Women whose self-esteem had been temporarily lowered were more receptive to the confederate's affection than were the women whose self-esteem had been temporarily raised. . . . The more intensely the individual needs approval, the more strongly she will reciprocate the other's feelings.

What this means to us, sisters, is that when you're feeling down on yourself, you're more apt to see a current unworthy partner as a potential partner. In fact, you'll probably make excuses for his clunker qualities. You'll tell yourself you're just being too picky. That he's really a nice guy. That you could never get anyone else!

But, of course, it doesn't last long. As soon as you feel better about yourself, you remind yourself the frog has just gotta go. The next time he's pouring his heart out to you—a quality you used to admire—you find yourself musing about what color nail polish you'll pick at your next manicure. When he stops to sensitively ask your opinion, you're stuck because, of course, you haven't heard a word he's said. It's moments like these that make you realize a ditch is in your immediate future.

You become irritated by the way he slurps his soft drink, the way he handles a wrong number on the phone, the funny little look he gets on his face when he wants to be intimate. And his pet name for you—the one that used to make your purr—now drives you ballistic.

Fred's nickname for me was "Boobette." (Don't ask me why. It's a long and boring story.) In any case, hearing his "Boobette" gave me the warm and fuzzies at first. Later it gave me cold, hard evidence that it was time to call it quits. Women, we know we're being unfair—but there's nothing we can do about it. We're female. It's in our genes!

Technique #13
Don't Be Fooled—Once a Frog, Always a Frog

Do not make the mistake, especially during moments of insecurity, of counting any unworthy partner's good qualities and making them a rationale for not breaking up with him or her.

Men, Get in Touch with Your Inner Coward

Men, for you, the realization that you must get all frogwomen out of your pond usually comes to you in a blinding flash, occasioned by one or more discoveries. The first and most obvious is that talking with her becomes torture. And listening to her becomes even worse. The third is that sex with the frogette is not worth suffering through the first two.

While we're on the subject, another sign from on high that you must split is while you're making love with her, fantasies of your old high school girlfriend Felicia start entering the scene.

Other apocalypses are when, at a party, you find yourself, instead of chatting up your current frog-date, preferring to talk with the insurance salesman you've just met. When these revelations start hitting you over the head, it's time to say, "Bye bye, frogettes." And dig up Felicia's phone number.

FEMALES ARE ASSERTIVE

However, gentlemen, I have to hand it to you. You're much better than women are at sticky situations, like telling old girlfriends that they are history. But then, society's strange acceptance of the (false) premise that you're the pursuer helps you out. (Actually, it's been documented that two-thirds of all romantic alliances are initiated by the woman.[6])

You probably don't realize it since, when you met any of the undeserving women you are currently dating, you may have been the first one to speak. Nevertheless, a serious research project proved that women actually make the first move. In fact, many do shameless things to encourage a man to make the approach.

In one particular study, the researchers set up hidden cameras in the ceiling of a singles party. They got all the action on film. Afterward, they sat around and watched the movie. Every time a man approached a woman, they backed up the film to determine what made the man approach one woman and not another.

Sure enough, the approached woman had given, as they called it, a *nonverbal solicitation signal*. What did the women do? Well, they smiled at the guy, danced alone to the music while eyeing him, flipped their hair or primped while continuing to eye the poor unsuspecting chap. Some actually looked right at him and licked their lips. Others winked and pointed to a chair, inviting their victim to sit in it.

Some of the more brazen ones slithered up to their target man with exaggerated hip movements. A few even sauntered right by the guy, patted his buttocks, turned back, and winked. You know, really subtle stuff like that. But the amazing truth is that because the guy was the first to actually say something, he thought he was the one who initiated the pickup. Women, this can work to our advantage. But men, it's to your detriment when the perpetrator is not a potential permanent partner.

So, gentlemen, if you have misgivings that you're being mercurial, forget it. No need to fear that at one time you were irresistibly attracted to the woman and now you're not. Chances are you were just subconsciously responding to some blatantly obvious (to everyone but you, that is) move she made on you. Think of yourself as a victim if it helps you make the break.

Nevertheless, you want to let the poor girls down gently. Since it's traditionally the man who asks for the date, you could simply stop asking them out. But have a heart. It could be that

TECHNIQUE #14
NO MORE "ONE MORE TIME"

Women, wipe out all thoughts of "well, one more date so I can let him down more gently." Gentlemen, forget "one more time" for auld lang syne. Say, "No!" to temptation and rise above your corporal cravings. Remember that this is your life we're talking about here, and you're never going to start UpDating if you keep going down with an ex.

some of your current dates have been harboring fantasies of sharing a life with you and growing old together. Such sweet dreams die a prolonged and painful death.

Watch out if any of them are the clingy, emotional type, as your announcement could entail weepy phone calls. Not only to you but to your best friends. The vicious ones could slash your tires. The desperate ones might knock on your door at midnight wearing a raincoat and nothing underneath. ("That doesn't sound so bad," you say. But beware, it drags you down into the frog pond again.)

Good-Bye, Old Frog—
Hello, New Prince(ess)

Now start preparing your mind, your body, and your spirit for a life of royalty. You may remember, I mentioned your surface and your substantial qualities, your cover, and your content. Perhaps you can't judge a book completely by its cover, but it gives a pretty good idea of what you'll find inside. That's why a hunting wardrobe and good grooming are necessary when you're tracking bigger game.

Whether it's fair or not, whether we like it or not, it's an irrefutable fact that when a superior potential mate spots you for the first time, "it" has already happened. He or she comes to a quick verdict—passing judgment on your clothing, your expression, your grooming, and how you carry yourself. He or she has judged your hairstyle and could probably tell you when you washed it last. Even your fingernails and shoes don't escape subliminal scrutiny!

You have already been categorized as a potential date or probable reject—based just on the way you look. The first few seconds you are reflected in his or her eyeballs are critical, consequential,

Technique #15
Glisten from the Get-Go

Don't expect to meet a spectacular potential partner
and start putting your best foot forward afterward. You
better be standing on your best hoof when you say,
"Hello," or you'll be in the reject pile before your
desired mate responds. Never ever underestimate the
pivotal power of his or her first gander at you.

conclusive, crucial, major, meaningful, momentous, heavy duty,
not to be sneezed at, and not chopped liver. (Can I say it any
stronger?)

If you still don't believe me, let's go to the videotape. The
Journal of Personality and Social Psychology published a study called
"Half a Minute: Predicting Teacher Evaluations from Thin Slices
of Nonverbal Behavior and Physical Attractiveness."[7] One by one,
college professors, high school principals, teachers, and students
saw thirty-second clips of individuals. From just that half-minute
glimpse on film, they were asked to predict how each person
would perform and how they would feel about that person several
months later.

At the end of the semester, the teachers, administrators, and
students were again polled on how they felt about each person
now that they had known them for a while. It was almost the
same.

People had guessed so accurately from having only seen thirty
seconds of the individuals at the beginning of the semester, the

researchers conducted a second study. They reduced the glimpse to just fifteen seconds. Still, amazing accuracy. Finally, they did a third study and showed the people only six seconds of other people. Many were *still* able to predict how they would feel about someone months later. Who says first impressions don't count?

Now obviously, the type of clothing you choose will differ depending on the type of partner you intend to hunt. We'll get into the various types of superior mates you might be setting your trap for later. But first a few more essential hunting tips that work with all royalty.

Ya Gotta Know da Habits of da Critter

When people ask me, "Who was your worst date?" or "Have you ever had a date from hell?" Butch is my answer. But Butch was something of a philosopher who, inadvertently, gave me some wisdom for the ages.

Butch was a blind date, and I should have known when he picked me up that this was not exactly going to be a dream evening. You see, Butch didn't come to my door and gently knock. At 7:30 P.M., our agreed-upon time, he honked his horn out in front of my house.

Dutifully, I ran out to his pickup truck. Well, on the way to the restaurant, we passed an open field. When he started to slow down, I began to fear for my safety. But he kept driving. When he said, "Wonder if the hogs have been rootin' it up in there," I feared for his sanity.

"I beg your pardon?" I asked. That was my mistake. Butch took it as a cue to try to regale me for the next hour and a half with stories of his passion, wild boar hunting. But all that listening was worth it as long as I could keep his contribution to philosophy of the Western world for the ages. Butch said, "If ya gonna make da kill, ya gotta know da habits of da critter."

If he'd ended it there, that would have been fine. But he spent the rest of the evening telling me about his acorn bait, and he was very proud he'd added diesel oil "so da dang flying coons don't go after it." He said sometimes he'd add raspberry Jell-O or beer to make it tastier for the hogs. And this was over dinner!

When he started telling me why a neck shot was better than an anal shot, I lost it and feigned a migraine. But looking back at it, the evening was worth his one terse philosophical verity: "If ya gonna make da kill, ya gotta know da habits of da critter."

Technique #16
LEARN SUPERIOR PEOPLE'S HABITS

Like Butch says, "Ya gotta know . . ." And if you're after Princely prey, ya gotta know what they eat, what they wear, where they vacation, how they speak, how they think. And much, much more.

Inspect Your Own Feathers

Just knowing that birds of a feather flock together isn't enough. You must take a good look at your own feathers and see if they measure up. Then you have a choice. Flock to friends with your own feathers—or get your feathers polished up. Fortunately, you can do that fairly easily. But first you must get rid of any preconceived notions such as "I am who I am, and they can take me or leave me."

The concept of "who I am" is a deeply philosophical one and one that I won't attempt to fully define here. Suffice it to say that who you are is a blend of genes, upbringing, life experiences, and habit. You can't change your genes or your history, but you can change your habits. And if you've been hanging with people unworthy of you, chances are your own habits could use a little luster. In other words . . .

You Gotta Be a Human Chameleon

Every one of the species God created has its own special unique characteristics. Birds can fly, monkeys can swing from tree to tree, turtles can carry their homes on their backs, fish can swim, and cats have incredible grace that gives them "nine lives."

But only chameleons and human beings have been blessed with one powerful quality that, to my knowledge, has no equal in the animal kingdom. It's the ability to change. If you want to capture a mate who is attractive, rich, principled, or wonderful in some other way, you may have to upgrade some of your thoughts, looks, or actions.

We all know that chameleons are able to change their colors to fit in with the environment wherever they wander. This is an enviable quality. But did you know that chameleons have an even more coveted quality? They can catch prey much larger than themselves. How do they do it? Scientists around the world once scratched their erudite heads over how chameleons accomplish this feat.

Even the world's reptile expert, Dr. Charles Louis Alphonse Laveran, the Nobel Prize–winning scientist who studied the trypanosomes of reptiles (don't worry—I don't know what trypanosomes are either), was flummoxed by chameleons' amazing ability to grab creatures much bigger than they are by just flipping their tongues. How they do it long remained a mystery throughout the reptile-obsessed world.

It was, however, common scholarly knowledge that the secret lay in the chameleon's tongue. Like most reptiles, its tongue's rough surface and sticky coating of mucus helps get a good grip on the target. But with other reptiles, this only works for smaller prey such as insects. If the rough-tongue technique is what chameleons used to catch large prey, they would need a humongous tongue with a huge surface. But they only have tiny chameleon-size tongues.

Finally, a couple of keen scientists from Belgium put their colleagues' consternation to rest by solving the great chameleon mystery of how the tiny critters could capture creatures way out of their league. The scientists took head-on shots using high-speed video cameras while the chameleons were tracking down their huge dinners.

The scientists discovered that the chameleon's tongue miraculously changed shape just before making contact with the prey, thus forming a kind of suction pad shaped a bit like a baseball glove. Once the suction cup had stuck to the big bird or other prodigious prey, the chameleon's tongue muscles contracted further, thereby tightening the suction cup. Chameleons were then able to enjoy their big dinner due to what the researchers dubbed the *flip 'n' suck technique*!

THE FLIP 'N' SUCK TO CAPTURE YOUR ROYAL

You, too, can use the flip 'n' suck technique to seize bigger prey. (This is not to be confused with you actually flipping over and sucking up to your potential mate.) It simply means you can flip some of your habits and suck in theirs. Then you'll fit in with their crowd to become an eligible mate for a Princess or Prince.

Like the chameleon, you must be a master of change, versatility, and flexibility. If your desired partner has an orange Mohawk, then it's time for a trip to your hairdresser for a spike cut and to your local drugstore for some heavy-duty gel. If your desired Prince or Princess is a preppie, head for Brooks Brothers

CHNIQUE #17

Become a Human Chameleon

Unfortunately, the "birds of a feather" law of nature still prevails with many human beings. Thus if we want a grade-A bird, we must start looking, sounding, and smelling like one.

for some preppie paraphernalia. If your desired mate is deeply spiritual, head for the nearest bookstore and immerse yourself in spiritual readings. And if your dream mate is an all-class act, you must curl your tongue as if it were born sucking a silver spoon.

Fake It 'til You Make It

Before you get the wrong idea, let me highlight that what you wear is just the veneer. Emulating exceptional people's style might initially unlock an exclusive door for you. But once you walk through that door, you've got to have the goods! That means the mind-set and the mores of the kingdom you're trying to infiltrate.

Wouldn't it be great if you could, simply by reading *UpDating!*, wake up tomorrow blessed with substantial social status, the beliefs, values, and tastes of those who were "to the manner born"? Also automatically have an excellent education, high social status, dynamite looks, and a strong sense of self? Dream on. It's not going to happen overnight.

Fortunately, however, there is a way. Those of you who have read my other books know that I am a dedicated defender of the "Fake It 'til You Make It" ideology. This will work in your quest for a first-rate mate as well. It's just that faking it is a little more difficult when you don't know what the "it" is. It's easy to say "act classy" to get a classy mate, "act honorable" to get an honorable mate, and so forth. But the upper echelon of class and character can sometimes be confounding. And unless we're "to the manner born," as they say, the "rules" can seem a little screwy. However, never fear—all will be revealed here.

Several years ago, I had the pleasure of speaking at an event where Les Brown, human potential mentor and author of the bestselling *Live Your Dreams*, also spoke. After hearing my presentation and having read one of my books, Les generously wrote me an endorsement, which he invited me to use. He said, "To be a winner, you've got to look like one, walk like one, and act like one. Leil gives you solid take-home techniques to be a winner."

And that's precisely what I'm going to do here. I'm going to tell you solid take-home techniques to be and get the type of superior partner you want. When you finish this book, you will have the characteristics of a Prince or Princess who can easily win the heart of a royal mate.

The "Location, Location, Location" Law of Love

So you've done the deed. Dud dates are now recent history—and you're ready for your marvelous mate to appear out of nowhere and fall madly in love with you, at which point the two of you will live happily ever after.

But there's a problem. Life is not a fairy tale. Like everything else you want, you've got to make it happen. What's the first step? If you're really, really serious about capturing a better partner, the first step is pretty drastic and not feasible for everyone. However, I promised you the truth, the whole truth, and nothing but the truth. So here we go.

To increase your chances of capturing prodigious prey, you may have to move! You heard me. In real estate, you've heard the old saying it's "location, location, location." Well, surprisingly enough, "location, location, location" is also a law of love.

Some years ago, a researcher examined the addresses on five thousand marriage licenses and put his results into a study called "Residential Propinquity as a Factor in Marriage Selection." The researcher, James Bossard, found that people usually tied the knot with someone living near them. In fact, 17 percent of couples lived within one block of each other. And a whopping 31 percent within four blocks. Only one-fifth of the couples lived in different cities.[8] It was obvious that most marriages occur between people who live pretty close to each other.

"Sure," you might say, "but that was then, and now is now. You forgot to take into consideration jet travel, more professional mobility, and the shrinking globe. Now it's a different story."

My answer: "Yes, it is—sort of!" True, we constantly come in contact with hundreds and hundreds of people—many more than just a few decades ago. But here's the sad truth. Even though your eyes lock with a dream date in a crowded airport and your heart skips a beat, what are the chances of your meeting? Or even if you do—and you share a preflight coffee—soon your heart's desire is soaring out of sight on one airplane and you're stuck on another. Wow, it was a dynamite fifteen minutes you spent together. But is that grounds for a big gamble in time and money to see if there was anything there?

Crossing Paths

Recently, precisely that happened to me. One evening I was racing like a white rabbit through an airport to catch a tight connection. As I bolted up to the counter clutching my purse in one hand and hauling my carry-on with the other, I realized I'd need my boarding pass and ID. I quickly and clumsily crouched down on the floor and dove into my purse. My wallet went flying in one direction, my makeup kit and a few embarrassing female accoutrements in another.

Voilà! I found my boarding pass scrunched at the bottom of my bag. Just as I was yanking it out, I felt a strong and gentle hand on my shoulder. A deep voice above me said, "Don't worry, ma'am, the plane can't go anywhere without me." I looked up into the face of our smiling and handsome pilot.

Blam! My throat went dry and my hands became moist. The sound of my rapid heartbeat covered the few inane remarks I mumbled. Roger, as I later discovered his name to be, extended his hand to help me up. While I scooped up the spillage from my purse, Roger explained that the aircraft hadn't yet arrived and we expected an hour delay.

I breathed a sigh of relief and, gathering my wits along with the residue from my bag, I let my eyes sneak a peek at his ring finger. Happily finding it naked, I lied that I was dying for a coffee and asked, "Is there a Starbucks nearby?" (I knew darn well there was one adjacent to the next gate.) My ploy worked, and for the next half hour, over a grande skim latte, I found myself falling hopelessly in love.

Then the plane arrived—much too soon. I shoved a business card at him, and he went to the cockpit. I went to seat 18D, and I never saw him again.

A few months later, my phone rang. It was Roger! He'd seen my picture in some obscure magazine advertising one of my books, and he called just to say hello. My fantasies went wild. Did that mean he felt the same? Couldn't be! But why did he call? I went through the whole ludicrous female litany of analyzing, over-analyzing, and then analyzing all over again.

By the way, gentlemen, we women do that. We can't help it. While you and the guy kid who lived next door were early male-bonding by tying your cats' tails together, your preteen sisters were female-bonding by discussing kids of the male gender in painstaking detail. They diagnosed every word a guy said. And what he really meant when he said, "Pass the mashed potatoes, please." They scrutinized every syllable, every expression, and every gesture for every nuance of meaning. When they finished, they reexamined it all again in case they missed something the first time around. It comes naturally for females. It's in our genes.

Anyway, Roger and I discussed which cities our work was going to take us to in the following months. Unfortunately, we discovered we wouldn't be coming within several hundred miles of each other. And neither of us was nuts enough to suggest a cross-country trip to meet again based on only those few minutes of flimsy evidence at Starbucks. Dreams dashed. Hopes vanished. That's the way our fast-paced world is these days.

More Proximity Proof

Let's take another scenario—one that holds more hope. Suppose you have more time with your potential partner. Let's say you are working on a month-long project and the man or woman of your dreams is flown in from another city to assist. Working so closely together in the office, your irresistible attraction to each other dawns on the two of you. Soon you're not just spending nine to five together, it's nine to six. Then nine to seven. One thing leads to another, and it becomes seven to nine, too. You're both in heaven.

But of course, the project eventually ends and so do your months of ecstasy. You go back to your respective coasts or towns. You talk for hours on the phone. You send E-mail daily and you make endless plans to get together. But you're both working hard at your jobs. Your phone bills become astronomical. E-mail becomes time consuming. Memories start to fade. The expense and inconvenience of a long trip starts to outweigh the pleasure of being together. And naturally, the gamble of packing everything up, giving up your job, and moving closer to your promising partner is just too big. So eventually, the happily-ever-after dreams filter down to "it was happy for a while."

Besides, that guy or gal you see every day starts hinting that you should have a coffee together. You do. Then it's dinner, then dancing, then you wind up doing it—and guess what? You've found yourself a new and faithful frog.

Familiarity Breeds Contempt—but Not in Courting!

Here are two of the most common scenarios when potential lovers who don't live near each other meet. You're sitting in an expensive café and see an exceptional person sipping a designer coffee. You smile. He or she smiles back. Then you both go diving back into your drinks. The guy thinks, "She's gorgeous. But do I dare make the approach? What if she was just being nice by smiling and she turns me down?" (Guys hate rejection.)

The woman thinks, "Wow, he's cute. I guess he'll come over to talk to me since I smiled at him. Of course, it's not my responsibility to make the approach, so I'll just sit here and wait." (Women hate being thought of as "aggressive.")

What happens? Zip! Your potential partner drives back to their upscale section of town, and you drive back to yours. Even if you do meet, it's not much different. Men, as you're chatting, you find yourself considering whether you dare ask her for a date. Women, you plot how to hint you'd like to go out with him. Should I or shouldn't I?

Let's say you've both decided in the affirmative and you make a date. You both have a good time on the date, so you plan another. And another. And maybe another. But each time, it involves (1) calling; (2) planning a place; (3) paying for a nice restaurant if you're dining together; and (4) deciding when, where, or whether you want to get together again.

If it falls into an affair, it's "My place or yours?" And that's complicated by "Who drives to whose place?" and "Who drives whom home?" and "Should we do it on weeknights since we both like to be in our respective bathrooms for our morning ablutions?" These are relatively minor challenges, but hassles nonetheless— compared to those faced by lovers who live in the same neighborhood. They can dine in the vicinity, do it, walk home, and look forward to doing it the next night, too.

The "Mere Exposure" Rule of Love

There is a proven phenomenon that greatly increases the chances of a love relationship developing. Psychologists have termed it, quite simply, *mere exposure*.[9] In short, this means that the more often you see a stranger, the more apt you are to establish eye contact. Therefore meet him or her. Therefore like each other. Therefore make a date. Therefore wind up together. The more times you run into someone by chance, the more apt you are to feel that you're destined to be together.

This was confirmed by researchers who surreptitiously arranged for men and women to "accidentally" run into each other a varying number of times.[10] At the end of the experiment, the researchers examined which of the subjects had formed friendships or love relationships with some of the others. They discovered that, all other things being equal, the people who met each other by chance the most often had developed the largest number of personal relationships. That means, if your potential partner sees you by chance several times a week, the likelihood of love is much better.

You may see the same dream date sitting in a chic café ordering cappuccino in the morning, lunching alone at L'Expensivo Restaurante, sipping tea at Hotel L'Elegance at four, working out at Fancy Zip Code Gym at six, and finally entering a posh charity event around the corner at eight. You will "be exposed" to your potential mate many times.

If you still don't believe how important where you live is, let's explore a study that proved it with powerful statistics. A group of researchers plotted the comings and goings of a number of singles in a town. Then they mapped the town into neighborhoods and drew a dozen or so expanding concentric circles emanating from each. They then tracked who married whom. Sure enough, there were more marriages within the smaller circles than in the larger ones. In other words, people were much more apt to marry someone who lived within a half-mile radius than someone who lived even a few miles away. This marrying-someone-close syndrome has become known to the great curious community of scientists as Bossard's law (after the researcher James Bossard, mentioned earlier).

Wait—that's not all! The more you run into someone, the more apt you are to have a successful relationship. Why? Because when you only meet in the more restrained structure of a date, you're only seeing the other person all gussied up and putting his or her best foot forward. Whereas when you see someone casually, say at the grocery store or the local coffee shop, you see that person more naturally. If you and Promising Potential Partner work together on an ongoing community project, he or she has a better chance of getting to know the real you. This fabulous person sees you interacting with other people: the grocery store clerk, the neighbors, your colleagues. Your casual meeting-by-chance con-

TECHNIQUE #18

LEARN THE "LOCATION, LOCATION, LOCATION" LAW OF LOVE

One of the best ways to capture Royal prey is to go live in their lair. Jog on the same paths, buy your toothpaste at the same pharmacy, shop for clothes in the same stores, walk your dog on the same streets, join the same gym, go to the same place of worship. Indulge yourself in all neighborhood activities. And keep in mind the new twist on an old rule, love thy neighbor: I say, "Let thy neighbor fall in love with you."

versations reveal a lot. And if you like each other in this more natural state, the chances are much better of your getting along on a long-term basis.

I have a girlfriend, Gillian, whom I've known since school. She, too, moved to New York and we saw each other quite often. At the time, we were both struggling to make ends meet. In spite of her near poverty, I always remember Gillian's expensive taste—but she certainly wasn't able to indulge it on her budget. We once were sitting in her tiny apartment drooling over the high-priced clothes in a fashion magazine. She spotted a beautiful pair of diamond earrings and an outrageously expensive Cartier gold watch.

She said, "Someday I'm going to have those earrings." But since we were going through a near-poverty period, we both decided to force it out of our minds. I easily forgot it but she didn't because she kept reminding me of the earrings and watch. It became a private joke between us. Every time we saw someone who looked very rich, we'd look at each other. She'd tweak her ear in memory of the coveted earrings. I'd smile and massage my wrist recalling the expensive watch.

Gillian soon became a fairly successful copywriter and eventually rented a beautiful spacious apartment in Queens, a borough of New York. To me, her life looked ideal. She was respected in her profession, traveled a lot, had a large circle of friends, lived in a beautiful apartment, and dated a lot. But now, because we were both so busy, we didn't have time to see too much of each other. Occasionally, I would talk to her on the phone and she told me that, yes, she was happy and everything was going well. But she complained that she didn't meet any interesting men—"just the same old crowd."

Then about a year ago, Gillian started talking to me about her biological clock, how it was ticking away, and she wasn't meeting any worthy candidates to be the father of her future kids. I knew Gillian had high standards and any candidate for that position would have to be a pretty good catch. At the time, I was just beginning to gather research for *UpDating!* and I told her about Bossard's law, or the "location, location, location" law of love.

A few months later, Gillian called me and announced she had found a new apartment. "Well," she told me, "it's not an apartment, really. It's a studio. In fact, it isn't really a whole studio. It's a tiny maid's room in a big apartment on Sutton Place" (which is one of the most exclusive sections of Manhattan).

When she told me the exorbitant rent she was paying for these tiny digs—far more than she had paid for her spacious two-bedroom apartment in Queens—I thought she'd lost her mind. "Why?" I stammered. I wondered what had gotten into her.

She replied, "Bossard's law!"

"Yikes," I thought. I was praying she hadn't made the move because of what I had told her. Life comes with no guarantees!

I visited Gillian in her tiny but classy little coop once or twice in the following months, and scrunched next to her on her miniature sofa, I really regretted her move that perhaps I was responsible for.

During this time, I was traveling a lot, so Gillian and I didn't have much time to even talk on the phone, let alone get together. Then just this January, I got a call from Gillian telling me she had some fantastic news but she would only tell me in person. She invited me to come over to her apartment. I confirmed the address of her building and we set a time. As we hung up, she said her apartment number was no longer E but Penthouse D. I assumed Gillian had moved to the maid's room in another apartment on the top floor.

I arrived at 6:30 and, in the elevator on the way up, I contemplated what restaurants in the neighborhood she and I would possibly be able to afford. The list was slim to nil. I knocked on the door of Penthouse D, and a maid, dressed in full servant's regalia, answered the door. I stammered apologetically that I was there to see Gillian.

"Yes," the maid replied. "Madam will be right with you." Madam! I wasn't here to see "Madam," I was here to see my good ol' girlfriend Gillian who, I figured, rented a small room in the huge apartment. Just then Gillian came running up to the door and gave me a big hug.

"Surprise!" she said. "Tonight when Gerald gets home, he's taking us both to dinner at Lutece." (Lutece, egad! I'd read about it—one of the best and most expensive restaurants in New York.) "But first, I have a present for you." She handed me a box with a stunning gold Cartier watch in it. It looked suspiciously like the one I'd lusted after so many years ago.

"Gillian, are you crazy? I can't accept this."

"Of course you can," she insisted. Then sweeping her hand around the room that was filled with beautiful paintings and exquisite antiques, she said, "I owe it all to you."

"You owe what all to me?" I sputtered.

"This *life*!" she responded. Then for the next half hour, Gillian told me everything.

How Gillian Got Her Prince

She said that soon after she moved in, about three times a week, she would ride down in the elevator with a distinguished gentleman named Gerald. They fell into conversation several times. It turns out Gerald was an art dealer who had recently lost his wife in a tragic accident.

One Saturday morning, Gillian was returning with a muffin she'd bought at the only affordable deli in the neighborhood. Clutching her little brown bag, she ran into Gerald coming out of the elevator. He said he was on the way out for brunch. Gillian crossed her fingers, did a quick 180-degree pirouette, and fibbed that she was, too. She then asked if he could, ahem, "recommend any good place for brunch."

Good going, Gillian! It worked—he invited her to join him. Well, you can guess the rest of the story. It's the classic "girl next door" tale that has repeated itself throughout history. The "location, location, location" law of love got Gillian her Prince. Fiction? No. Fact! It is a fairy tale with a happy ending. And how many of those do you hear these days?

Gillian's List

So where are the best grounds to stalk Royals? That, again, depends on the type of partner you are seeking. If you are a

> ## TECHNIQUE #19
> ## RESIDE SMALL, BUT THINK BIG
>
> You don't need to break the bank to move to a neighborhood where a pack of prestigious potential partners live. Just take a smaller pad in their vicinity and you're much more apt to bag bigger game.

Hunter or Huntress of a high-class or rich mate as Gillian was, here are a few suggestions.

Since the concept of class is only whispered about, you must dig deep. H. L. Mencken in the *American Mercury* created a list of social indicators. You could, of course, get a copy of *Who's Who* and see where a preponderance of the important populace lives.

You could also try for the zip code subscription list of the *Atlantic Monthly* and rent a room in that zip code. An easier way to decide where to hunt is to judge the importance of the newspaper in the town. That's an excellent social indicator, and the *New York Times* tops the list.

Some of the cities where Gillian would have made out well are, in alphabetical order, Baltimore, Boston, Chicago, New York, Philadelphia, and San Francisco.

Pursuing wealthy mates is a bit more difficult in the countryside because it's challenging to track them down in their mansions. However, an abundance of them hide out in the expensive and expansive rural terrain of Connecticut, Massachusetts, New York State, North Carolina, Pennsylvania, and Virginia.

> ### Technique #20
> ## Migrate Near Your Preferred Birds
>
> Give it some good hard thought. What type of a bird would you be happy flying with for a lifetime? An honorable one? A gorgeous one? A creative one? A rich and classy one? Figure out where they nest, and fly there ASAP.

So how do you judge if a venue is *not* conducive to making a quality kill? I've been told that the places where you are least apt to find classy people are locations that have (would you believe) a preponderance of bowling alleys. In fact two class watchers made a list of cities that "regrettably" had the highest number of them per capita.

Digging Deeper

You can find even deeper reasons for making your zip code match that of the lifetime partner you want. When you live in a community and mingle with the residents, you begin to take on their ways of looking at the world. As if by osmosis, their beliefs begin to blend with yours. Their philosophy of life, attitudes, and way of acting all begin to take effect on yours. You find yourself seeing things in a different way—their way. Thus you develop the all-important similarity.

Gillian wanted a "classier" Prince, so she moved into a "classier" neighborhood. But if your definition of a dream partner is one who is more educated, perhaps you'd move near a university. In that way, not only would you run into educated people, but your outlook on life would become more academically oriented. Thus you would be more attractive to those in a more learned society.

If you seek a deeply devout partner, you might move into a worshipful community. There you would see life through a more spiritual lens. Thus you would be more attractive to those whose lives are dedicated to the God of their understanding.

If it's an artistic mate you seek, you might even move into my run-down neighborhood in New York. In Soho you'd find hundreds of starving—but very talented—artists. If it's not a Lutece cup of tea you crave, as Gillian did, but herb tea in a cracked cup at one of the local holes-in-the-wall, c'mon down!

Due to space limitations in this book, I must choose only a few types of Royalty as examples. Since (1) "good looking or gorgeous," (2) "high class or rich," (3) "honorable," and (4) "creative or interesting" topped the list of the most-in-demand partners, I offer techniques to capture those four. Many of the techniques will work on all types of Royalty. Simply dub in your preference. Now we'll get on with the four types topping the Most-Wanted List.

3 How to Find a Drop-Dead Gorgeous Mate

The Challenge of Capturing a Beautiful Princess or Handsome Prince

When your definition of your desired partner is one who is drop-dead gorgeous, a host of problems arises. Not the least among them being (1) your own insecurity, (2) their suspicions of your affection, and (3) their screwed-up psychology having had to carry the burden of being so beautiful. (Yes, I'm serious.)

Many of us are completely confident chatting with practically anybody, anytime. But when we come face-to-face with a stunner, the cat gets our tongue. We stutter, we stammer, we make complete fools of ourselves.

I've been there, done precisely that, and like everyone, kicked myself afterward. One time a tall handsome hunk followed me around at a convention. I was so suspicious of his motives that I found myself hating him! (I hated myself a lot more later when mutual friends told me he was sincerely interested in me.)

Unfortunately, at first, looks are the determining factor with most people. A study called "Importance of Physical Attractiveness in Dating Behavior" gave us this bad news.[11]

Three hundred seventy-six college men and women signed up to go to a dance with a blind date. Unbeknownst to the subjects, the investigators had secretly and callously rated them on their physical attractiveness. All of the participants then filled out a personality test. The researchers told them they were going to be paired off with "someone with a similar personality."

The researchers lied—all in the name of science, of course. They really just hurled the participants' names into a hat and paired them off randomly with no consideration of looks or personality. However, everyone attending the dance thought the researchers had matched them up because they had a similar character.

After the dance, the researchers asked each student to complete a brief questionnaire giving their opinion of their blind date. They answered questions like, "How much did you like your date?" and "Would you like to see this person again?"

When the researchers compared the results to the bogus personality test, it turned out that only one factor affected how much the person liked their date: how good looking he or she was. Yes, Virginia, looks count.

What If I'm Not a "Looker"?

One of the most common questions is, "Do I have a prayer capturing a gorgeous partner if I'm not too terrific looking myself?" There is good news here. It's a resounding "Yes."

The reason many people don't go for a fabulous looking mate is that they think they can't! There is a big psychological block that I call the *out-of-my-league factor*. Everyone has an opinion of him- or herself and what type of date he or she "can get." As we'll soon see, most people's self-image is way out in left field. We seldom see ourselves as others see us.

In another study, ruthless researchers had a group of folks fill out a questionnaire asking how attractive they thought each other individual in the group was.[12] They then asked each participant two questions:

1. How do you think everyone else in the group rated your attractiveness?
2. How attractive do you feel you are?

The participants' answers to these two questions were quite similar. In other words, people's assessment of their own looks and what they surmised others thought of them were almost identical. However, there was an enormous disparity when comparing their answers to what others *really* thought of their looks. Most people had rated a participant as much better looking than he or she thought she was.

The subjects were pretty good at ranking the other participants' looks. Nevertheless, when it came to their own, they were

TECHNIQUE #21
DON'T ASK YOUR MIRROR

When it comes to how good looking a partner you can get, you're probably way off base. It's been shown that most people grossly underestimate their own attractiveness. Go for the gorgeous potential mate with confidence. You'll be surprised!

way off base. A few plain-old, regular-looking folks thought they were ravishing.

However, most subjects erred in the other direction. They truly were good looking—and everyone else in the group judged them so—but they thought themselves to be unattractive. Many participants even rated themselves the least attractive person in the group!

What's this got to do with us getting a gorgeous partner? A lot, because most of us only go after people we think we can be successful with. Since both men and women underestimate their appearance, they are hesitant to pursue someone they feel is much more attractive. Yet it's been shown that we are terrible judges of our own looks, and we grossly underestimate our attractiveness.

Another factor enters the bizarre story of love and beauty. That is, although we may find someone objectively good looking for a date, we may not find them attractive as a lifetime partner. A lot more comes into your choice of a partner when you're considering waking up staring at that face every morning for the rest of your life!

With continued contact, our opinion of someone can change. If you truly know that looks are not your strong suit, here is some advice: avoid mixers, singles parties, and the like, where people make snap judgments only according to your looks. Get involved in an activity, like volunteer work or taking a class where you have continued contact with fantastic potential mates.

Whose Looks Are More Vital: A Woman's or a Man's?

In my relationship seminars, I often ask, "Which do you think: Are a woman's looks more important to a man? Or are a man's looks more important to a woman?" After hearing a cacophony of variations on "a woman's looks are more important to a man," I ask them to take another guess. They say, "What, a man's looks are more important to a woman? No way!"

Surprisingly enough, a man's appearance matters more to a woman than vice versa. However, objective good looks are higher on the male wish list. That sounds contradictory but here is the explanation. A study called "Radiating Beauty: The Effects of Having a Physically Attractive Partner on Person Perception" dem-

TECHNIQUE #22

REMEMBER—BRAINS BEAT BEEFCAKE

Gentlemen, still worried that you're not a "10"? Forget it. Even for a gorgeous Princess, it's more important for her future kids that Daddy is bright rather than Daddy is a beefcake.

onstrated that if a man has a gorgeous woman on his arm, the world considers him richer, more accomplished, and better looking.[13] That's why many men, especially the less secure ones, only choose stunners to show off.

Women are more into the character in a man's face—and they are more particular! If you take one lucky man and line up one hundred women of appropriate age, socioeconomic status, and education, if the circumstances were right, he could probably get it up sexually for a majority of them. Now, line up a hundred men and this time it's ladies' choice. The results? Although most of the guys in the lineup are attractive, only a few of them would really ring her bell. Why? Because a woman is far more specific in what she is seeking. If she wants a man with character, your face must reveal character to turn her on. If she values sense of humor, you'd better have some credible laugh lines. If intelligence is her big turn-on, having a good head on your shoulders will be more important to her than a good-looking one.

This desire for a man's intelligence even carries over into how a woman likes a man to dress. One study showed that women preferred a man when he was wearing glasses to when he was not.[14] Not so, vice versa. Doesn't that prove that women go for an intelligent look over just another handsome face?

Here's the Skinny on Getting a Gorgeous Partner

I could say it in one word—and I will: *self-confidence.* So many people are intimidated by fantastically striking men and women that they don't approach the stunners. They figure everyone else is making a move on them.

Guess what? It's not true. From my experience as a Pan Am flight attendant (in the days when it was a glamorous profession and most flight attendants were knockouts) and as a model, many of my gorgeous friends were dateless on a Saturday night. Why? Because men were afraid to make the move on them, figuring they didn't have a chance. Women suffer the same severe shyness with handsome men.

For more on this—and a cure—see the last chapter in this book.

Why He or She Digs That Turkey (and Not Me, f'Instance)

Why does one person push your buttons more than another? Psychology? Biology? Anthropology? It's really all three.

It's understandable that married couples resemble each other in age, religion, ethnic background, socioeconomic status, and even political views. However, a group of researchers were thunderstruck when they discovered that four times higher on the similarity scale were people who had married look-alikes![15]

It doesn't always have to be someone who obviously resembles you. Often it's subtle. In one study it was discovered that many husbands and wives were similar in hidden physical details, like the length of their earlobes, the distances between their eyes, and even the length of their fingers. The explanation for this is that we all have what sociologists call *sexual imprinting*.

Our experiences between the tender ages of five and eight lie forever dormant in our subconscious. Psychologists now realize that the major part of our personality comes from these early childhood experiences. These recollections resonate through our psyches so strongly that they even determine our sexual preferences. The deeply buried memories we have of security and love most often come from family members who loved us when we were little tykes.

These loving folks often look like us. After all, who was around when your sexuality developed? Daddies, mommies, uncles, aunts, brothers and sisters, and others swimming around in the same gene pool. Therefore, twenty, thirty, forty, fifty years later, when we see someone who has a family resemblance, incipient feelings of love start to percolate.

That's why a man or woman can be turned on by one person and not another—even if the other is better looking. Granny had a good answer to that conundrum. Whenever I'd express my astonishment that one of my girlfriends had fallen "for such a turkey," she'd simply nod her head and philosophically decree, "Love will go where it's sent." She didn't know she was thus echoing Pascal's wisdom of more than three hundred years ago: "The heart has its reasons, whereof reason knows nothing." (For those of you who can't trust anyone over three hundred, this means that people flip over people for no darn good reason.)

But there is a reason. Mother Nature doesn't just poke your potential partner one morning, point at you, and say, "Honey, that's the one for you." Mother Nature doesn't demand that the sound of your voice, the way you laugh, or the way you look at her with soulful eyes will make her heart falter, hands perspire, and feet tingle or make your stunner ask you which way to the altar. There is a scientifically sound reason love at first sight happens.

I experienced this firsthand with a roommate when I was modeling clothes. I had just moved into a great apartment that had a balcony and, on the first floor, a little eatery and bar called Thursdays. Because the apartment wasn't cheap, I needed someone to help pay the rent. I searched on the roommate board at the agency and called one woman who had advertised.

My new roommate turned out to be a lingerie model who had the same name (Jessica) and frame as the gorgeous 'toon in the movie *Who Framed Roger Rabbit?* Most evenings, after she'd had a long hard day in the showrooms, Jessica and I would go down to Thursdays because they gave us free drinks and munchies.

The manager there was no fool. He knew that many of the male customers patronized Thursdays just to get a glance of Jessica slithering in, hips swirling, just like she was on the runway. No highway crash ever rivaled the rubbernecking that followed Jessica wherever she went. When she arrived, every man's eyes widened in excitement and every woman's narrowed into green catlike slits of jealousy. More than once I wanted to shout, "Bartender! A saucer of milk for every woman in the house, please."

One evening I was sitting at the bar munching a hamburger with my 36C-24-35 roommate. A very ordinary-looking guy of medium height, with dry brownish hair and tiny eyes a tad too close together, said with a big grin, "Excuse me, ladies. Do you believe in love at first sight? Or do I have to walk by again?"

Jessica swung her head around expecting to blow him off as she had done half a dozen others that evening, especially ones with dumb lines like that. But this time, when Jessica's eyes met his beady little ones, she froze momentarily. Then she turned the revolving stool toward him, tilted her head, and lowered one shoulder. She crossed her legs seductively and said, "You could try."

He shrugged, smiled, and turned to walk back into the crowd. Jessica looked like a locomotive had hit her. Lest he leave and not return, Jessica called after him, "Uh, just kidding."

"I was hoping you'd call me back. Hi, my name is Fausto," he said, confidently extending his hand, which Jessica willingly took. "And you must be the lovely Jessica I've heard so much about." Turning to me, he asked (with less gusto), "And your name?" while still holding Jessica's hand.

After a few minutes, I managed to disappear, unnoticed by either, into the crowd. Occasionally, I would glance over at them. Once Fausto and Jessica were toasting their glasses. Another time

TECHNIQUE #23

BEWARE THE BURIED GENES BUTTON

So do you have to be drop-dead dazzling to win the heart of a beautiful Princess or handsome Prince? Absolutely not. The reason unbeknownst to both of you is that your genes might just happen to push your target partner's buttons.

Jessica was laughing and dusting real or imagined lint off his jacket. The last time I saw them that evening was as they were walking out the door together, destination unknown.

Later, much later, I was awakened by the apartment door opening. A giddy Jessica stumbled in. She was trying to be as quiet as possible, but her hiccups gave her away. I mumbled, "Where have you been?"

"What did you, hic, think of him?" she asked.

"Who, Fabian?" I asked.

"No, silly, hic . . ."

"Flavio?"

"No. *Fausto!* Isn't he, hic, cool?" Fortunately, half asleep, I could feign drowsiness to avoid answering.

Jessica and Fausto had a stormy relationship for about six months until he finally broke it off. Apparently, she wanted him to commit, and he wanted to play the field for a few more years before taking the big step.

Once, in the sad days after they split, I was helping Jessica extract all pictures of Fausto from her photo album. As she turned

Technique #24

Don't Sweat the Insecure Prince

Women, this is not just sour grapes. It's been proven that the guys who go only for looks are less secure. This type of male needs the extra prestige that having a stunner on his arm provides. Studies support this. Secure men go for personality over pretty every time.

a page, I saw a shot of a man standing by an antique car. I said, "Wait, you missed one."

"No, that's not Fausto," she replied. "That's my dad when he was younger." Jessica had always spoken about how much she loved and missed her father and what a close relationship they'd had.

However, it wasn't until that moment that I knew what he looked like and made the connection between her dad and Fausto. I realized retroactively why Fausto fit Jessica's love mandate. He looked just like her father!

Science is now fully aware that drugs can sway the brain's emotional chemistry—for example, by selective serotonin uptake inhibitors like Prozac and Paxil. Scientists have discovered they can also define love in terms of chemical reactions. You can't make someone love you specifically by giving him or her a pill. But chemical reactions result from visceral reactions to past events and persons.

That does not mean that when Jessica spotted beady-eyed little Fausto with his hackneyed pickup line she thought of her dad. At least, not consciously. In fact, in most cases, people don't make the connection. Nevertheless, incipient feelings of love come from deeply buried responses to sharp cuts of pain or pleasure axed in our brains at an early age.

Now here's some good more news for women who rank (or think they rank) lower on the looks scale. Researchers conducted a study called "Focusing on the Exterior and the Interior." The control group consisted of two personality types of men. The first group of guys tailored their behavior to whomever they were talking with. In other words, they acted one way with one person and differently with another. They dubbed these men *self-monitors*. (I call them *two-faced*.) The other half of the control group was men who were more consistent in dealing with people. They were surer of themselves.

The researchers asked every man in the study the same question before they fixed them up on a date. "Would you prefer a date who is not terribly physically attractive but is really quite nice? Or would you prefer an attractive woman who is not very nice?"

The result? The less secure subjects chose to go out with the good-looking woman who was not really nice. The more secure subjects opted for the one with nice qualities rather than physical good looks.

This means that the type of man most women would want opts for qualities over looks. The only problem with this, of course, is that it takes a longer time for a man to assess a woman's qualities, whereas her facade is instantly conspicuous.

Before I continue with how to handle your gorgeous new partner once you've enticed him or her, I want to clarify something. This is not just speculation. They are all demonstrated techniques, both physical and psychological, to help you win the gorgeous man or woman of your dreams.

Please don't misunderstand. None of them eclipse the brutal reality that the better looking you are, the better chance you have of getting a gorgeous mate. I merely want to show that it is not written in stone.

Do you remember the story of the "Little Engine That Could"? With every turn of its wheels, it said, "I think I can. I think I can." It's the same in getting a looker as your lover. Go for it! Don't think you don't have a chance because everybody else is pursuing him or her. You'll be surprised at your success. And if one of them turns you down, don't let it dampen your determination. There are lots of lookers out there, and if that's your heart's desire, you'll get one.

However, the methods of winning one are a little different from getting another type of superior partner. Here are some rules.

Flattery Won't Get You Anywhere with a Looker

It started with Dale Carnegie of *How to Win Friends and Influence People*. You want to get in cozy with someone? You butter them up. For some seventy years people have been saying "amen" to that like they heard it in church. They think it's as basic as the law of gravity. But it's not! With a gorgeous partner, it could have just the opposite effect.

That's not to say great-looking people aren't suckers for compliments just like everyone else. Yet there's a difference. Chances are, the beauties are so used to people blowing sunshine up their tush that it loses its effect—unless it's done right!

Suppose tomorrow you're going through your E-mail or listening to your phone messages, and one of them is from her majesty, the queen of England. She has invited you to be introduced to her at the palace, all expenses paid, of course. First you will be officially introduced in front of the court. Then just the two of you will retire to her chambers, sip high tea, and sit around to chat the rest of the afternoon.

Perhaps your first reaction would be the same as mine. I'd clap an astonished hand to my forehead. Then I'd slump, keel over, and hit the floor. My first thought, after I came to, would be "Eeek! What do you say to a queen when you're all alone, eyeball to eyeball?" Maybe you could study up on the early dos and don'ts and hack the "How do you do, your majesty" part. What then? Chatting up a queen is quite different from shooting the breeze with your buddies.

Of course, once you and the queen become really chummy, you and she will probably start jabbering away like magpies, giggling and chatting about almost anything. However, at first, there are a few dos and don'ts.

Likewise, when casually conversing at first with a beautiful woman or a handsome man, you should heed these few early directions.

Don't Swoon Too Soon

The host introduces you to a dazzling man or woman at a party. Before you've uttered "hello," you've already fantasized the two of you falling madly in love, having long evenings of romantic dates and even longer nights of passionate sex, getting married, vacationing around the world together, then settling down to decorate your new mansion—and maybe having three kids, two dogs, and an iguana and living happily ever after.

It's difficult, but as you smile across the room at this gorgeous specimen of humanity, try to understand that he or she has no idea that you're hallucinating a lifetime together. In other words, you must treat this magnificent human being just like anyone else.

This is not just an admonition from an embittered girlfriend of mine who loved and lost—all in twenty-four hours. It's been shown that fawning doesn't work with a gorgeous person. Let me tell you what happened to a fellow flight attendant who swooned too soon.

My friend Ginger was not only outlandishly beautiful and bright, but she was also an accomplished flirt—therefore an infamous heartbreaker. Ginger's passion happened to be gourmet dining, although you'd never know it to look at her willowy figure. Ginger was no dope. She'd discovered a way to dine free in the best restaurants in any of our layover cities. How did she do it?

Ginger's modus operandi on the plane was to glance at the left hand of any male passenger she fancied who was traveling alone. Her prey was usually perched in the first-class section of the plane. "Paupers don't fly first class," she liked to say.

Whenever she'd spot her soon-to-be dining host for the evening, she'd really lay it on. More times than not, the passenger would fall for it and ask her out. Naturally, she would then go into her well-rehearsed act of, "Oh, I've heard the [such 'n' such—i.e., read "expensive"] restaurant is terrific." She would thus hoodwink her passenger pawn into taking her there.

Ginger adored the dinners, and the male passengers adored Ginger. Her only problem with this smiling-for-dinners tactic was wriggling out of a second date. Ginger, being as gorgeous as she was, could afford to be very particular. Sadly, so far, no one she dated had the attributes to qualify him as a Ginger-quality Prince.

Then along came Prince Donald. He was a passenger on an overseas flight we both were working. I saw Ginger do a double take when she spotted him reading his paper in the first-class lounge of the 747. I thought, as they chatted, that he was just the latest victim of Ginger's dinner ploy.

But apparently Donald profoundly affected Ginger. Donald was tall. Donald was handsome. Donald was witty and articulate. Donald looked educated and intelligent. And obviously Donald was no pauper.

Ginger came running back to the galley to tell me of the prize quarry she'd just spotted.

"Do me a favor, Leil. I tried three times but couldn't see his left hand, and I don't want to be obvious. Would you just casually walk by him for me and see if he's wearing a ring?"

It took me two or three times up and down the aisle, but finally I spotted that his left-hand ring finger was naked. I went back to the galley to herald the good news. Ginger was waiting, her hands folded and her head down in mock prayer.

"No wedding band—not even white ring skin," I announced. (Traveling married men on the prowl have a nasty habit of slipping off their wedding bands—but it always leaves a white sun-tanless ring on their finger.) "I pronounce him single," I said.

"God is good," she mumbled. Ginger then put on more lip-stick, fluffed her hair, and went into full siren swing with more gusto than I'd ever seen. She smiled. Donald responded. She flirted. Donald fell for it. And, just like all the others, they made a date.

I'd usually be asleep in the hotel room when Ginger returned from one of her fine dining experiences. I'd hear her come in, glance at the clock, see it was about 10 or 10:30, and go back to sleep. This particular night, however, when I glanced at the clock as she came in, it was 12:30 A.M.!

"Ginger, are you all right?" I asked.

"Just fine," she giggled. I could tell Ginger was more than fine. "And Donald's from New York, too! How lucky can a girl get?" were her last words before she fell into an optimistic and slightly intoxicated slumber.

On our flight home the next day, Ginger told me the whole story. In a nutshell, "Everything went beautifully," she said. I joked about it being a role reversal for her when she confessed she spent a good part of the dinner telling him how special she thought he was.

I was certainly no relationship expert then, but my instinct told me she might have gone a bit overboard telling him of her admiration.

Sure enough, our next flight together, I asked, "How is it with Donald?" She gave me a deadpan look and a tight smile, then quickly looked away to disguise her distress. "He never called," she blurted out. It was obvious Ginger did not want to talk about it. My suspicion that she had gone overboard with early declarations of her admiration was confirmed.

Interesting thing about stunning people. Since they are excep-tionally desirable, they don't fall prey to the fawning we mortals find so flattering. If someone falls in love with us at first sight, most of us don't mind at all. It's a compliment. For a gorgeous catch, however, it's just, "Ho-hum, another day, another worshiper."

If your spectacular-looking prey has the slightest suspicion that your praise is dishonest or for self-serving opportunistic reasons, it can be disastrous to the relationship.

A doctoral dissertation (with a typically baffling name: "Reactions to Evaluations by Another Person as a Function of Self-Evaluation and the Interaction Context") showed that desirable people are unfazed by compliments.[16]

The researcher demonstrated that if you compliment people who suspect you have ulterior motives—like wanting their money or their body—they won't like it. And they won't like you! Since extremely rich or beautiful people are accustomed to others wanting something from them, early compliments have little effect. In other words, praise is a gift horse whose mouth beautiful people examine very carefully!

What this means to Hunters and Huntresses of love, is that we should not give effusive compliments to a good-looking person right off the bat. In fact, if you know you're going to have continued interaction for some reason (like working together, volunteering for the same project, having the same friends, being in a class together, and so forth), a possible tactic is to feign disinterest.

The study showed that good-looking people will be more receptive to someone if he or she is actually cool toward them initially. Then as the person gets to know them, their admiration grows.

Here's how they proved it. Researchers introduced participants in the experiment to people called *evaluators*. To make the results of this experiment clearer to understand for our purposes, I'll call the subjects "lookers" because they were all drop-dead

Technique #25

Start Slow, Then Let It Grow

Someone who doesn't get a lot of compliments is a much bigger sucker for them than the person who always gets praise. And the person who is continually complimented gets a ho-hum attitude toward them. The trick is to start by appearing supposedly oblivious to the spectacular looks of your potential partner. Then let your affection and admiration appear to grow and grow—gradually. Good-looking people want to feel you appreciate them more for their other qualities than their drop-dead looks.

knockouts. I'll call the participants *wanna-be lovers*, or *wanna-bes* for short.

The researchers arranged for a group of lookers to individually meet a new wanna-be lover several times. After the first meeting, the lookers were permitted to "eavesdrop" on the wanna-bes' conversations about them. The group of wanna-bes discussed whether the gorgeous person each had met seemed intelligent, likable, interesting—or dull, ordinary, and a host of other negatives. What the lookers didn't realize was that the wanna-bes were part of the experiment and directed to say either complimentary or derogatory things about them.[17]

Then the dynamite-looking people had a second and third conversation with the wanna-bes. Again the gorgeous folk got an earful of the wanna-bes' comments. They didn't know that the researchers had directed the wanna-bes to express opinions scripted by the researchers and not necessarily true. Each group of wanna-bes had to follow one of four sequences.

1. **Stating an initially positive impression, turning to negative.** Start out saying positive things about the looker after the first meeting but have it turn to negative after several more meetings.
2. **Stating an initially positive impression, staying positive.** Start out saying positive things about the gorgeous Royal after the first meeting and continue saying positive things even after getting to know each other.
3. **Stating an initially negative impression, turning to positive.** Start out saying negative things about the looker initially but turning it into a positive evaluation after a few subsequent meetings.
4. **Stating an initially negative impression, staying negative.** Start out saying negative things about the looker after the first meeting and continue having a negative impression even after getting to know each other better.

After the gorgeous subjects had eavesdropped on all the wanna-bes' conversations, the researchers reversed the roles. Now they asked how much the gorgeous Royals liked the individual wanna-be lover who had judged them.

The researchers were shocked that the attractive people liked the wanna-bes best who had started out with a negative first impression of them but then turned positive after they got to know each other. In fact, they liked those wanna-bes even *better* than the ones who said pleasing things about them at first and continued to compliment them. This means that good-looking people want you to appreciate them for their personality, not from first impressions of their looks.

Another surprise was that the gorgeous Royals even liked the wanna-bes who had a negative impression of them first and negative later. In fact, the lookers liked them more than the wanna-bes who liked them at first but whose affection tapered off after getting to know each other. It makes sense. We like people whose admiration for us grows as we get to know each other better. This is especially true of great-looking folks. They are so accustomed to people falling all over themselves when they first meet that they find it refreshing to meet someone whose admiration slowly grows with continued exposure.

The significant point for you in your hunt for superattractive people is that they like to feel that they earned your respect. They like you best if you don't fawn at first but grow to respect and like them with continued contact. They can be downright turned off if you start out by going overboard with flattery followed by a gradual tapering off of expressions of your admiration.

Unfortunately, this is much too common a situation. You've heard the phrase "You always hurt the one you love"? One reason is that often we start making our loved one feel like a million dollars. Then little by little, we let down in our praise. As the studies prove, that hurts most of all.

If, however, you've already met your gorgeous potential partner and you've started saying how wonderful he or she is, keep it up! As you get to know each other better, don't neglect to keep the strokes coming. If you started strong and it's working, keep pouring on the praise. However, as I said, it's even better if you began with faint praise. Then you can keep raising the volume—slowly!

Now here's another biggie when dealing with a stunner. If you are going to compliment him or her, you'd better make sure it's true! False flattery gets you thrown back in the frog pond quicker than anything else.

A group of spectacular-looking individuals filled out a self-evaluation of their strengths and weaknesses. Then a group of subjects (wanna-bes) complimented them on qualities the lookers valued in themselves, and other wanna-bes complimented them on qualities that the lookers did not feel they had.

You got it! The false flatterers found themselves in the reject pile immediately. So make sure when you praise your looker that it's real—or at least real in their self-concept.

I Love You for the Reasons You Love Yourself

Here's a technique that some naive souls might think is tricky. But I exonerate you from any guilt in using it because (1) it helps solidify your relationship, (2) you are not lying in any way, and (3) it is a lovely thing to do for someone you love.

Here's how it works. You start by saying to your stunning potential mate, "I was reading a book the other day [true] that was talking about the various things that people want to be remembered for in posterity [also true]."

Some people want to be remembered because they could make everyone laugh. Others because they brought themselves up by their bootstraps. Still others want to be remembered because they were exceptionally kind to everyone.

Then tell your potential mate what you are most proud of in life. You must be truthful here. However, unbeknownst to looker, this is just a way to soften her or him up to tell you the truth.

The next step is to ask, "What are you most proud of in life? What would you like to be remembered for in posterity?" Then listen—carefully. Remember all the details of what your potential mate is telling you.

Now here's the tactic. Don't say a word about it for a few weeks. Try to let your prospective partner forget what she or he

Technique #26

Tell Your Stunning Royal, "I Love You Because . . ."

Tell your great-looking potential partner, "I love you because . . ." and then fill in his or her reason for loving him- or herself! When drop-dead gorgeous people feel you love them for the essence of who they are—and not just for their looks—they feel they have found the right partner indeed. Do it! It's for your mutual happiness and for bonding with a beautiful partner.

ever told you. Then at an opportune moment you'll say, "The reason I really admire [or love] you, dearest, is because . . ." Then fill in the quality he or she is most proud of! Embellish it if you wish, but stick to the central theme.

For instance, suppose your stunner has said that the quality she is most proud of is that she is kind to everyone. Then you say, "The reason I really love you is because you are kind to everyone you come in contact with." Then, if you wish, add more, like, "I saw how kind you were to the waiter who spilled your coffee last week." Or, "When we were at that party, I saw how kind you were to your colleagues and even that chatty woman who kept bugging us. And that little old lady you gave your seat to . . ." blah blah blah.

Can you fathom the profound effect this has on someone? It's powerful. You see, Princes and Princesses are used to being admired for, say, their prestige, their money, their good looks.

But when someone recognizes their magnificence in an area they secretly feel magnificent in—wow!

We are all seeking someone who loves us for ourselves—the essence of who we are, if you will. When you were a baby, if you were fortunate, your parents loved you not because you were rich or famous or talented or witty or even gorgeous. They loved you, well, because you were you. It's no different with gorgeous people. Their parents loved their little Princes or Princesses just because of their existence.

We are all seeking to replicate that love.

How to Capture a Rich or "High-Class" Mate

Class *Is Not a Dirty Word*

When I asked students in my relationship seminars, "Who is your ideal partner?" or "What type of superior person are you seeking?" the answer that shot out of their mouths most often was, "A higher class of person" or "Someone with class."

Now herein lies a problem. We live in a country that pretends class doesn't exist. As sociologist Paul Blumberg wrote in *The Predatory Society*, class structure is "American's forbidden thought."[18] In fact, most of us think it's classless to even admit that classes in our democratic country exist. (The irony of it is that those at the rock bottom and those at the tippy-top of the class ladder openly and shamelessly proclaim, "Of course class exists!")

But here's where it gets interesting. Each "class" defines it differently. Ask someone at the bottom of the social ladder what class is, and he or she will ruefully say, "It's the 'haves,' the big shots who are rolling in it, the fat cats who live on Easy Street." In short, they think class is simply how much money you have.

Ask someone in the middle, and the word so horrifies them that they stutter and stammer. After an abject denial that class exists in our democracy, and that of course they are not in the least bit conscious of it, they reveal (in hushed tones lest someone overhears them) that they think money has something to do with it. But they suspect that education and profession are also involved.

Now, at the top of the heap, like at the bottom, the upper class says unabashedly, "Surely class exists." The difference is that the uppers define it in terms of values, taste, style, behavior, and ideas. Naturally, they admit, it helps to have money and education to be included in the designation "high class." But it's hardly a crucial element.

Since, unlike the United Kingdom, we lack the convenient system of inherited titles, ranks, and honors, there is bad news and good news. The bad news is that our concept of class is almost impossible to define and we are hypocritical about it. The good news is that, in America, we have more class mobility than anywhere else in the world.

My beloved homeland, America, is officially hypocritical when it comes to class. Our democratic government, while insisting all people are equal, has a cut-and-dried system of government employee inequality. Those high-level administrators at the top grade of eighteen look down their prestigious noses at those below, like, say, the fourteens. Peering farther down their noses they spot the fives (secretaries), twos (mail clerks), and ones (messengers, etc.). Even among themselves, the high-teen–grade feds have a class order. The eighteen-grade feds can ask the purchasing department for a teak desk. Those below them can only request mahogany. Another step down, and they're stuck with walnut.

Sadly, the lower teen–rated feds can't ask for anything better than oak. Spoken? No. Undisputed? Yes.

By the way, class or pecking order is not strictly an adult concept. *The Journal of Personality and Social Psychology* revealed a strange phenomenon that happens whenever two or more kids get together.[19] Just like chickens on a farm, they form a pecking order of popularity. If you ask kids from the first grade on up, "Who are the top kids, who are the bottom kids?" they rattle off a litany of names as easily as they sing the alphabet.

I deeply admire this official myth of classlessness, but for the sake of helping you find your classy partner, I'm not going to mince my words. I refuse to bow to the politically correct. I'm going to call it like it is. You and I may not agree with all of the manners, mores, and cultural tastes of Easy Street residents and we may think them silly. I only pass them on as ammunition if you're out to bag an old-moneyed mate.

So What's "Classy"?

Since to most, "classy" connotes wealth, status, intelligence, integrity, and even good looks, our dream partner is going to be rich, prestigious, good looking, smart, and honorable. In short, classier. If the qualities you seek in a classy mate differ, I leave it to you to choose from this list or substitute your own specifications.

When scouting for higher-class mates, most of us (myself included) are unaware of the subtleties that reveal whether we are worthy of them or not.

Here's an analogy. When you cut a lemon in half to see if it's good, you inspect the skin, the seeds, and the pulp. Finito! However, a biologist is far more discerning. Sure, he takes a passing glance at the skin and seeds, but that's just the beginning. His sharp eyes examine the carpel wall; the placenta; the vesicle; the pedicel; and the endocarp, exocarp, and mesocarp. (I don't know what those are either.) By then, if the placenta isn't solid, that lemon lands in the laboratory garbage disposal. The poor lemon never knew why it was trashed.

Same thing can happen to us. A high-class person can trash us, and we'll never know why. We may have meticulously groomed ourselves, dressed to the nines, and even brushed up on our Ps and Qs. Still, that's just the skin of the lemon. The uppers are far more sensitive and look much deeper before considering you as a potential mate.

Unfortunately, we can't go to night school to get a Certificate of Class, and, as far as I know, universities don't offer degrees in Posh. I had to learn it in the school of hard knocks (to my ego). I'll try to pass on here what I learned, to save you the excruciating pain of the plethora of sympathetic smiles and raised eyebrows that I suffered.

As we've said, similarity is a big determinant. A classy person quickly picks up on whether you're "one of them"—not just by what you say but by how you say it, how you pronounce it, and how loudly!

This type of refined individual tends to judge your table manners. Many calculate your class by what time you eat dinner, what cocktail you drink, and—would you believe it?—what flavor of ice cream you crave. They judge you on how your living space looks—down to where you position the TV and what accessories you have in your bathroom.

The list goes on—your interests, your hobbies, what magazines you read, your front door, even your toilet paper! Subconsciously, nothing escapes their judgmental sensitivity. So be prepared for some big eye-openers.

Of course, classy prospective mates are sensitive to how you dress and cut your hair. Still, surprise surprise, grooming is not number one on their list and a chic hairstyle is not necessarily cool

Technique #27

Get Real About "Class"

Here's what a very bright but blunt call-it-like-it-is friend of mine said to me when I told her I was uncomfortable talking about what's classy and what's not: "Get real, Leil. You're acting like you're writing a book on how to be a serial killer. Everybody knows class exists in America, and anybody who doesn't is full of . . ." (And here she used a very *un*classy word that, literally taken, means the excrement of male cows.) To capture an "upper-class" mate, you first must admit that class exists. After all, high-class people do!

in their kingdom. The bottom line is, the slightest gaucherie on your part could prevent you from being their mate.

A Touch of Class

Just like a DNA expert can tell all about someone simply by looking at a toenail sliver, an upper is aware of whether you're an all-class act by the most confounding trivia. Their mores are mind-boggling. It's not the big or obvious things that indicate class. For example, an expensive shiny car does *not* suggest class. A neatly trimmed lawn does *not* look upper class. And expensive liquor is *not* the chosen libation on Easy Street. Most of us, unless we're born with a silver spoon in our mouth, might think just the opposite.

When I was a flight attendant, I was dating a wonderful man who was my definition of a Prince in every way. Although I believed Ken to be a "starving artist," he was wise, creative, and very kind. I'll be forever grateful to him for the jaw-dropping insights he and his mother gave me about what's class and what's crass.

I'd been journeying through my life for several decades completely confident that, no matter who I should meet, I'd be up to snuff. I was successfully recuperating from my severe case of youthful shyness and emerging, I thought quite well, into a sophisticated young adult. I mean, I had good table manners, and whenever I met someone, I let them know how "pleased" I was to meet them. Of course, I was friendly, wishing practically everyone "a nice day." With the help of Mama's good training and a few Amy Vanderbilt books on my shelf, I felt I could eat at anyone's table and not raise an eyebrow. I also had a pretty good wardrobe, which included some fairly expensive clothes with the designer's name right on them to prove it. Let me tell you of one of the first times I went out with Ken.

How Many Mistakes Can You Find?

As a fun How Classy Are You? test, see how many mistakes you can find which revealed that I was not in his elevated class. There are twenty-three bloopers—at least twenty-three I know of now.

The first time I invited Ken to visit, I knew he was going to be impressed with my apartment, which I had recently renovated and refurnished very tastefully. As you approached my front door, you'd see two potted plants placed symmetrically on each side. On the door, my apartment number, "Seventeen Eleven," was spelled out in elegant cursive script on a plaque.

My apartment had wall-to-wall carpeting in the bedroom and some brand-new Oriental rugs that I'd just bought at the rug outlet. I was especially proud of my new twenty-one-inch TV (which at that time was huge) in the living room. On the bookshelf, I had the impressive Great Books series, and I'd placed a copy of *National Geographic* and *Scientific American* on the coffee table to show my eclectic interests.

I was especially looking forward to showing Ken the display of wine glasses I'd purchased around the world on my flights and a few from a collector's catalog.

I hoped Ken would ask to use my bathroom because it was newly furnished for comfort and elegance. In addition to Dacron towels embroidered with my initials and squiggly gold threads sewn into each end, I had a matching toilet seat cover and curved rug. If he should happen to lift the toilet seat, my Prince would see a small sea of pine-scented turquoise water.

Ken was coming over to my apartment Saturday afternoon. When he arrived, I refrained from asking him if he wanted the fifty-cent tour (which even I knew was uncouth). However, after he'd gotten an eyeful of my beautiful living room, I was determined to lure Ken into the kitchen on some pretense. I asked him to come in and have one of the delicious biscotti, which, I jokingly told him, I had swiped from the plane. The real reason was that I wanted him to see my spanking-clean kitchen with all the conveniences—a dishwasher, a microwave, and an electric stove—all of which I was buying on time, of course. I'd even had the cupboards redone in beautiful beige Formica. Right in the center of the kitchen table, I had lovingly placed a vase of chrysanthemums.

Sitting there, drinking tea and nibbling on the five-finger discount biscotti from the plane, I smilingly asked Ken how he liked my apartment. At that instant, I detected a sick expression spread across his aristocratic face. Choking on his biscotti, he said, "Uh, very interesting, Leil." (Looking back at it, knowing what I know now, I was lucky I didn't lose my Prince that very night.)

During that year, my starving artist and I became very close. He wasn't making much money on his art but that was not important. Though he was relatively poverty-stricken, I loved Ken and we became engaged.

That November, my starving artist invited me to his mother's home for Thanksgiving dinner. He'd told me not to dress up. So I stuffed myself into my favorite Jordache jeans, zipped them up with a wire hanger, and donned my vintage Coca-Cola T-shirt with "It's the real thing!" written on it.

When Ken arrived, he took one look at me and gently suggested that perhaps I might want to change. "To what?" I asked surprised. "You told me not to dress up."

When he saw my confusion, he said, "Uh, may I?" He was asking if he could look in my closet. He pulled out some old gray woolen slacks that were unraveling at the seams, a high-collared white cotton blouse, and a slightly moth-eaten beige Shetland sweater. I assumed he wanted me to wear these old clothes because of his parents' poverty. They lived in New Jersey, and I fully expected to be traveling to a hole-in-the-wall tucked away in a crowded Newark neighborhood.

As we drove to New Jersey in Ken's old Plymouth, we passed the bustling city. Slowly the panorama became more verdant and countrified. Finally, we turned down a long, winding dirt road that seemed to go on for miles. Bumps in the half-graveled road made me wonder what kind of shack we were traveling to. Continuing down the dirt road, we drove by several fenced expanses of grass where beautiful Thoroughbred horses were grazing.

The only person we passed on the road was a woman on horseback dressed in full regalia—hard hat, jodhpurs, riding jacket, and boots. When she saw Ken's old car approaching, she stopped, skillfully dismounted, and, holding her horse by the reins, came up to our window. "Kenny," she exclaimed, "it's been so long. How good to see you!" He and his equestrian friend exchanged pleasantries for a few moments and then Ken introduced me. "How do you do?" she asked.

I didn't quite know how to answer her question. "Uh, fine," I said. "And how about you?"

She laughed and, after a few more moments of chitchat with Ken, said, "Good-bye." I told her how nice it was to meet her. She smiled at Ken and off she rode.

As we continued down the lane, which had a clearly British name, we started passing beautiful mansions placed well back from the road. Then we turned into a smaller twisting beige gravel lane. I could barely detect a huge manor at the end of it. At this point I expected Ken would drive right past it to some servants' quarters beyond the house to see his "Mummy."

But no, he drove right into the large circular gravel driveway, and we stopped a few yards from the front door. I was thunderstruck when it hit me that perhaps this was his parents' house. My jaw flopped around in a feeble attempt at speech, but I only produced a pathetic squawk that sounded like, "Duh-duh-do your parents live here?"

At that point he took me by the hand and led me through the door to a life-changing experience.

It turned out that Ken was from an extremely upper-upper-class family, "old money," as people would say. For decades he had tastefully hidden the fact from his artist friends. I was probably the first friend that he revealed his very unhumble beginnings to.

His mother gracefully descended a long staircase, extended her hand warmly, and said, "How do you do? Kenny has told me so much about you." I was glad she added that second sentence so I wouldn't be faced with answering that perplexing "How do you do?" question again.

Ken's mother was a remarkable woman, and over the next several years, she and I became very close. (On a deeply tragic note, Ken was later killed when his Cessna 150 crashed. I'll never fully recover from that, but life goes on.) In fact, Ken's mother and I are still friends today. I owe many insights I'm about to share with you about the American Royal lifestyle to the most wonderful Princess I've ever known, "Mummy."

During those few years, I had the opportunity to observe how the world looks from the top of the class totem pole. I saw what people erroneously call "living on Easy Street." Although Ken and I didn't choose to reside there, I learned what it's like. With my tongue firmly implanted in my cheek, I pass these discoveries on to all who have aimed their arrow at the heart of a "high-class" partner.

Decorating Your Pad to Impress a Royal

Looking back at my middle-class digs that I was so proud of, I now understand why Royalty would roll their eyes. Let me excerpt the earlier smug description of my newly furnished apartment, verbatim. However, this time I'll number the twenty-three boners that betrayed me as more of a proletariat than a Princess.

You will remember that I wrote *and whenever I met someone, I let them know how (1) pleased I was to meet them.*

Here's where my verbal problem began. I discovered that the uppers never say, "Pleased ta meet cha" (even if they pronounce it more royally). Rather, they say, "How do you do." Now, understand, this is not a question that requires a logical response. It is merely the soothing noise uppers make, almost simultaneously, upon meeting each other.

When Ken's upper-class neighbor said to me, "How do you do," I was coarse enough to actually answer her! I responded, "Uh, fine. And how about you?" (No wonder that occasioned her nervous laughter.)

So how should you respond when they say, "How do you do"? The uppers, like parrots, nonsensically respond by repeating precisely the same words, "How do you do." Period, no question mark.

To add to the assault on Ken's neighbor's silver-spoon sensibility, I later said, (2) "Nice meeting you." No, no, Leil. It should have been simply, "Good-bye." Not "So long," "See you later, alligator," or the pretentious Italian "Ciao," which is pronounced "chow" as in grub. Upper-class people crisply and clearly say simply, "Good-bye." Even on the phone, as the conversation finishes, they suddenly sing, "Good-bye." (Not even "Good-bye now.") Then click, the line goes dead.

Of course, I was friendly, (3) wishing practically everyone a nice day.

Another painful pea for uppers. I learned that the "nice day" mentality is decidedly middle class. However, today it is extremely prevalent and well intended. When someone wishes you a nice day, I suggest you simply give in and say, "You, too." (Resist the temptation to say something sarcastic like, "Thank you, but I have other plans.")

Apparently—and this disturbs me—the "smile for everyone" culture that I teach in my seminars is also a middle-class mark. Never mind—I defend it.

I also had a pretty good wardrobe, which included some fairly expensive clothes (4) with the designer's name right on them to prove it.

Save that. We'll get into Royalty-hunting regalia, big-time, a little later.

The first time I invited Ken to visit, I knew he was going to be impressed with my apartment, which I had recently renovated and refurnished very tastefully. As you approached my front door, you'd see (5) two potted plants placed symmetrically on each side.

Wrong! This must have been the first sign to Ken that he was not entering the palace of a Princess. Symmetry is out at the top! Having two potted plants placed in the same position on each side of the door is just too neat and not terribly creative. A classy person probably would not have even had one potted plant outside the door. Nevertheless, if he or she did, it would not be balanced by another.

In fact, high class people would decree any sort of symmetry—such as equal side curtains pulled back from the window or a lamp placed exactly in the middle of a table centered against the wall—to be "motel-room motif." Supersymmetry says you're trying to prove how orderly you are.

Another clunker was (6) my choice of flowers. Can you believe that the upper class actually has a pecking order of plants? This may be going too far, but for scholars fascinated by class or floral minutiae, here it is:

Looking around your digs, an upper would admire your bouquet of tiger lilies, amaryllis, clematis, columbine, and roses—unless they were bright red! In that case, you slip down a class or two in their estimation. In fact, anything red (my favorite color) is pretty proletariat. Red tulips, which I've always loved, are an upper-class no-no. Other classless flowers are poinsettia, chrysanthemum, zinnia, gladioli, begonia, dahlia, and the poor petunia.

Inside the house, the more out of season the flowers are or the greater distance they've traveled to reach your home, the better. To really impress the upper class, dig deep into your pockets for exotics like anthuriums, Oriental lilies, Hawaiian heliconias, birds-of-paradise—or anything else from around the world. (Read "rare and expensive.")

On the door, (7) my apartment number, "Seventeen Eleven," was spelled out in elegant cursive script on a plaque.

Oh, dear—another no-no. Too pretentious. A simple 1711 would have been more in keeping with the style to which, at the time, I wished to become accustomed.

My apartment had (8) wall-to-wall carpeting in the bedroom . . .

Where did I go wrong there? Sounds nice, huh? That's what I thought, too. For starters, high-class Royals would never choose wall-to-wall carpeting. They prefer to place their genteel feet on parquet, hardwood, or stone. They feel, "Who in their right mind would want to cover up anything that beautiful?"

. . . and (9) some brand-new Oriental rugs that I'd just bought at the rug outlet.

Ouch! Royalty consider the words *brand-new* and *Oriental rugs* to be oxymorons. The only permissible covering for their expensive floors is *old* Oriental rugs—the more threadbare, the better. Why? Age connotes value, and they can say, "It's been in the [old-moneyed] family for a very long time." Anybody with an ounce of blue blood flowing in their veins would have averted their eyes from my very déclassé new Oriental rugs.

I was especially proud of my (10) new twenty-one-inch TV (which at that time was huge) in the living room.

That gaffe could fill an entire humiliating chapter. Bad enough to have a large TV, but putting it smack dab in the living room is unpardonable. You see, the more conspicuous your television, the more unclassy you are in your potential partner's eyes. In fact, the tippy-top uppers have no TV, or, if they do indulge in the nasty secret habit of occasionally watching a program, their TV is tiny and totally out of sight.

If you're like 99.99 percent of the population who loves the tube, hide it. Or tell your upper-class friend that it's just a closed-circuit monitor for the stock market or Sotheby's auction house.

On the bookshelf, I had the impressive (11) Great Books series, and I'd placed a copy of (12) National Geographic and (13) Scientific American on the coffee table to show my eclectic interests.

Nice try, Leil. (Hey, it wasn't like I had the *National Enquirer* on my table.) However, it turns out that both of my display publications were, according to a renowned class watcher named Stuart Chapin, middle-class accoutrements. In fact, he broke popular periodicals down into a class-status list. Following, updated, are lists of representative rags.

Low Class (from lower-lower up to bordering on middle)
National Enquirer and that entire genre
"Girlie" magazines (except an occasional forgivable
    Penthouse or *Playboy* for bachelors)
Popular Mechanics or any magazine having to do with cars
Cosmo, Good Housekeeping, and almost any other women's
    magazine
Any sports magazine with the possible exception of those on
    golf or tennis

Middle Class (from lower to higher)
Reader's Digest
Martha Stewart Living
National Geographic
Golf, tennis, or boating publications
Scientific American
The New Yorker
Most all travel magazines with a few exceptions describing
    exotic (read: expensive) destinations

Upper Class (from lower-upper to upper-upper)
Atlantic Monthly
NY Times Book Review
Town and Country
New York Review of Books
Times Literary Supplement (London, of course)
Paris Match
Hudson Review

When trying to impress a classy Royal, garnish your coffee table with these "upper-class" publications closer to the top.

I was especially looking forward to showing Ken (14) the collection of wine glasses I'd purchased around the world on my flights and a few from a mail-order catalog.

Apparently, collections of anything—unless each individual item is a true work of art unto itself, like Peruvian Mola or pre-Columbian masks—are an embarrassment. Don't ask me why. It's just one of those things. Perhaps the reason my cheap wine-glass collection was so pathetic was because the unwritten caption was, "Ha ha, look where I've been and you haven't."

Even more pitiable was the fact that I'd gotten some of them from mail-order catalogs. Apparently, anything ordered from a collector's catalog, except country or sportive clothes, is blatantly bourgeois. At least it wasn't as bad as a matchbook collection or Royal Doulton figurines, Hummel statues, or Beatrix Potter character figurines.

In the "darn lucky I didn't have that in my living room" list are any heraldic items such as a family coat of arms, a needlepoint canvas imprinted with a college seal, or a family tartan. Although any subtly visible ties to "Mother England" are good through uppers' eyes, any obvious ploy to prove your connection instantly sends you plummeting downward.

Additionally, the privileged class avoids anything with their names or initials engraved, embossed, or printed on it. Well, they might go so far as writing their name in a book just so any borrower will know where to return it. However, you won't find a bookmark with "John Smith, his book" anywhere in the house.

I hoped Ken would ask to use my bathroom because it was newly furnished for comfort and elegance. In addition to (15) Dacron towels embroidered with my initials and squiggly gold threads sewn into each end, I had a (16) matching toilet seat cover and curved rug. If he should happen to lift the toilet seat, my Prince would see a small sea of (17) pine-scented turquoise water.

My spanking-clean, fancily furnished bathroom would occasion the rolling of Royal eyes. My Dacron towels with gold threads were obviously on the proletariat list of favorites. Then, there were my initials (already defamed earlier) for users of my bathroom to admire.

The upper class furnishes their bathrooms for comfort, certainly not elegance. The facilities are merely to pop in and out of as quickly as possible when nature dictates. Oh, upper-class bathrooms are hygienic, all right. (After all, one of the "servants" cleans them daily.) But they are not showplaces.

In fact, an old-fashioned toilet seat in a dark varnished wood is much classier than plain white or, heaven forbid, a cover (especially fake fur). No blue-green pine-scented water is used to disguise the purpose of the toilet. (Yes, uppers use the word "toilet," not euphemisms like "powder room," "restroom," "john," or "potty," the military "latrine," or the cutesy "little boys' or girls' room.") You'll find no matching rug or sanitary little circle to absorb any dripping from wet feet or other regal extremities. Nor will you find any fake flowers, pictures, magazine racks, or gadgets in an upper-class latrine. A Waterpik is stretching it. And, of course, any bathroom humor (like jokes on wall plaques or written on toilet paper, or nude female figures painted under the lid cover for the sole salacious pleasure of urinating males) is unthinkable.

In short, the bathroom is not a showplace in uppers' houses. Rather, it's strictly utilitarian.

I was determined to lure Ken into the kitchen on some pretense. I asked him to come in and have one of the delicious biscotti, which, I jokingly told him, I had (18) swiped from the plane. The real reason was that I wanted him to see my spanking-clean kitchen with all the conveniences, (19) a dishwasher, a microwave, and (20) an electric stove . . .

The fact that upper-class households lacked these kitchen conveniences made me scratch my head—until it was explained to me that only uppers' servants enter it. Royalty have very low-tech kitchens with a minimum of labor-saving appliances, like garbage disposals and their stoves are gas, not electric.

(21) . . . all of which I was buying on time, of course.

Most of us normal folk occasionally have to buy things on time. Nevertheless, if you do, don't tell your upper-class partner about it. It's just not done on Easy Street.

I'd even had the cupboards (22) redone in beautiful beige Formica.

You goofed again, Leil. They should have been wood. No Formica in a classy kitchen.

Right in the center of the kitchen table, I had lovingly placed a vase of (23) chrysanthemums.

You already had the seminar in symmetry and flower hierarchy. I failed both courses.

Sitting there, drinking tea and nibbling on the five-finger discount biscotti from the plane.

Need I say where I went wrong here? Uppers wouldn't lift a sugar pack from a restaurant table even if they knew their cupboard was bare.

I smilingly asked Ken how he liked my apartment. At that instant, I detected a sick expression spread across his aristocratic face. Choking on his biscotti, he said, "Uh, very interesting, Leil."

Now I understand!

So, how did you do? Did you catch all of them? If you didn't, don't feel bad. Most of us "normal folks" wouldn't. But, if you're really serious about bagging an upper-class mate, study up on this esoterica.

Technique #28
Let Your Digs Convey Class, Not Crass

Lest you be influenced, chuck any home-furnishings magazines with photos of modern kitchens, wall-to-wall carpeting, glistening bathrooms, and symmetrical floral displays. Hide your TV, all collectibles, most magazines unless they're foreign or literary, and anything with your name or initials on it. Give your home the following checkup to determine where you now stand on the class totem pole.

How Classy Is Your Home?

Three eminent class scrutinizers put together the following scale to calibrate the class standing of your living room.[20] Go ahead and take the test (but make sure your tongue is firmly implanted in your cheek as you do so).

Begin with a score of 100. For each of the following in your living room (or those of friends or acquaintances), add or subtract points as indicated. Then ascertain social class according to the scores at the end.

> Hardwood floor (solid wood)—Add 4
> Parquet floor (solid wood)—Add 8
> Stone floor—Add 4
> Laminate floor—Subtract 4
> Vinyl floor—Subtract 6
> Wall-to-wall carpet—Add 2

Shag carpet—Subtract 4

Working fireplace—Add 4

Gas log fireplace—Subtract 5

New Oriental rug or carpet—Subtract 2 (each)

Worn Oriental rug or carpet—Add 5 (each)

Threadbare rug or carpet—Add 8 (each)

Ceiling ten feet high or higher—Add 6

Cathedral ceiling (with or without skylights)—Subtract 5

Original painting by internationally recognized
   practitioner—Add 8 (each)

Original drawing, print, or lithograph by internationally
   recognized practitioner—Add 5 (each)

Reproduction of any Picasso painting, print, or anything—
   Subtract 2 (each)

Original painting, drawing, or print by family members—
   Subtract 4 (each)

Windows curtained, with rods and draw cords—Add 5

Windows curtained, with no rods or draw cords—Add 2

Window blinds, mini, plastic—Subtract 2

Window blinds, mini, metal—Subtract 1

Window blinds, mini, wood—Add 1

Window blinds, vertical—Subtract 3

Wooden venetian blinds—Subtract 2

Metal venetian blinds—Subtract 4

Genuine Tiffany lamp—Add 3

Reproduction Tiffany lamp—Subtract 4

Any work of art depicting cowboys—Subtract 3

Professional oil portrait of any member of the household—
   Subtract 3

Any display of collectibles—Subtract 4

Transparent plastic covers on furniture—Subtract 6

Furniture upholstered with any metallic threads—Subtract 3

Cellophane on any lampshade—Subtract 4

Ashtray—Subtract 4 (each)

Refrigerator, washing machine, clothes dryer in a room for living—Subtract 6

Motorcycle kept in living room (unless inner-city loft)—Subtract 10

Periodicals visible, laid out flat:

> *National Enquirer*—Subtract 6
>
> *Popular Mechanics* or any vehicle-related periodical—Subtract 5
>
> *Reader's Digest*—Subtract 3
>
> *National Geographic, Time, Newsweek, Life*, etc.—Subtract 2
>
> *Smithsonian*—Subtract 1
>
> *Scientific American*—Subtract 1
>
> *Town and Country*—Add 2
>
> *New York Review of Books*—Add 5
>
> *Times Literary Supplement* (London)—Add 5
>
> *Paris Match*—Add 6
>
> *Hudson Review*—Add 8
>
> No periodicals—Subtract 5

Family photograph (black and white)—Subtract 2 (each)

Family photograph (color)—Subtract 3 (each)

Family photograph in sterling silver frame—Add 3 (each)

Potted citrus tree with midget fruit growing—Add 8

Potted palm tree—Add 5

Fresh-cut flowers—Add 3

Artificial flowers (plastic)—Subtract 5

Artificial flowers (silk)—Subtract 3

Bowling ball carrier—Subtract 6

Fishbowl or aquarium (fresh water)—Subtract 4

Fishbowl or aquarium (salt water)—Add 1

Fringe on any upholstered furniture—Subtract 4

Identifiable Naugahyde aping anything usually made of
  leather—Subtract 3

Any item exhibiting words in an ancient or modern foreign
  language—Add 7

Tabletop obelisk of marble, glass, etc.—Add 9

Fewer than five pictures on walls—Subtract 5

Furniture more than fifty years old—Add 2 (each)

Bookcase full of books—Add 5

Overflow books stacked on floor, chairs, etc.—Add 6

Hutch bookcase (wall system) displaying plates, pots,
  porcelain figurines, etc., but no books—Subtract 4

Wall unit with built-in TV, stereo, etc.—Subtract 4

TV, stereo, etc.—Subtract 6

Piano (grand or baby grand)—Add 4

Piano (upright)—Subtract 1

Computer—Subtract 3

Fax machine—Subtract 4

On coffee table, tiny object from funny or anomalous
  place—Add 1

Work of sculpture, original, but not made by householder or
  any family member—Add 4 (each)

Work of sculpture made by householder or any family
  member—Subtract 5 (each)

Item alluding specifically to the United Kingdom—Add 1
  (each)

Item alluding, even remotely, to Tutankhamen—Subtract 4
  (each)

Framed certificate, diploma, or testimonial—Subtract 2 (each)

Laminated framed certificate, diploma, or testimonial—
  Subtract 3 (each)

Item with a tortoiseshell finish, if only made of Formica—
  Add 1 (each)

Eames chair—Subtract 2 (each)
Recliner—Subtract 3 (each)
Recliner sofa—Subtract 4 (each)
Sofa with hidden compartments—Subtract 5 (each)
Anything displaying the name or initials of anyone in the
   household—Subtract 4
Curved moldings visible anywhere in the room—Add 5

Your Class Score
245 or above: Upper class
185 to 244: Upper-middle class
100 to 184: Middle class
50 to 99: High proletariat (working class)
Below 50: Mid- or low proletariat (lower class)

I promise you, a low score is not social suicide. It just means
you might want to hide a few things before you invite your high-
class prospect over for dinner.

The Classy Car—It's Not What You'd Think!

Let us move from your domicile to your auto. Your Cadillac or
Rolls would not impress the high class. Neither would your Mercedes. Uppers would call the latter "a sign of high vulgarity, a car
of the kind owned by Beverly Hills dentists."[21] The upper-uppers
own a boring, blandly colored, heavy old Oldsmobile or Buick or
even a Jeep. The subtext of these types of cars is that their mansion is so remote that the winding roads leading to it are not
paved.

Car decorations? Heaven forbid! You won't find baby shoes or
foam dice hanging from the rearview mirror or Saint Christopher
statuettes stuck to the dashboard. No self-congratulatory bumper

stickers inform everyone "I brake for small animals" or brag that there's a "baby on board." Nor do uppers' cars have stickers commanding other motorists to vote Republican or Democrat or to "honk if you love Jesus."

When you double-date with a classy person, be prepared for a possible unusual seating arrangement. The first time I went out to dinner with Ken and his parents, his father was driving. We all walked together to the car. Ken's father opened the door for his wife, and, much to my surprise, Mummy got into the back seat.

I blurted out, "Oh, I don't mind riding in the back." A knowing smile crossed all three of their patrician faces as I was assured that everything was fine. Ken got into the back seat with his mother, and his father helped me into the front seat next to him.

I later discovered the class-decreed seating arrangement for the automobile. When riding with another couple:

- **Lower class.** The men sit in the front, the wives sit in the back.
- **Middle class.** One couple sits in front, the other sits in the back.
- **Upper class.** Mixie-matchie! A woman sits with the husband or date of her friend in the front seat, and the other two opposite-sex individuals sit in the back. Kinda kinky—but fun, huh?

I also learned mixie-matchie pertains to dinner parties. At an all-class table, you don't get the security of sitting next to your partner. The assumption, of course, is that the two of you have such wonderful social graces that you can converse comfortably with (or ignore confidently) anyone you get stuck sitting next to. Besides, you're with your classy mate so much anyway, why not take a minivacation from each other?

Technique #29

Don't Drive Flashy Wheels

An almost universal male fantasy is picking up his Princess in his flashy car and having her swoon. Not going to happen! At least not with an upper-class Princess. "Too showy," she'd snort. The only exciting thing about your car should be the mixie-matchie seating arrangement.

Speaking of family proximity, if you're tired of having to visit relatives, rest assured when you marry Royalty that visiting relatives will not be a problem. In fact, upper-class people usually flee from relatives and prefer to travel alone with their spouse to exotic places.

Problems can arise when marrying across class lines. Ken had an uncle named Chaddwick, who was equally aristocratic, equally honorable, equally creative, and, of course, equally rich. Like Ken after him, he also was a fugitive from the rich lands of New Jersey who opted for a "real life."

Chaddwick chose to escape—not just a few hours away by car, but a few hours away by plane across the country. He settled in the then hippie-chic Haight-Ashbury section of San Francisco. There he took up with a beautiful bohemian sculptress named Shantral, who had been born with a marijuana joint rather than a silver spoon in her mouth.

Never having experienced the drug culture, Chaddwick had assumed that "getting stoned" was having rocks thrown at you, "tripping" was going for a weekend jaunt, being "potted" was for plants, a "stash box" was where kids put their allowance, and "grass" was something the servants cut.

For a short time, he enjoyed the thrill of life with Shantral and her high-flying friends. He went to early Jefferson Airplane and Grateful Dead concerts. He drank Kool-Aid spiked with LSD at Ken Kesey's forest home. He went to scores of share-ins, be-ins, and love-ins. He and Shantral joined "love circles" of friends who flew kites, tossed Frisbees and flowers, painted designs on each other's backs, and had all imaginable body parts pierced. He laughed at the *San Francisco Chronicle*'s gross exaggerations of the "acid freak" who took a swan dive into the front of a truck moving at 70 miles per hour. And of love-in hippies lying in a field staring at the sun until they were permanently blinded.

Soon, however, the exhilarating dream began to turn into a nightmare. His friends told him chilling stories about ecstatically feeling like ravens, or Jesus Christ, or people six inches high.

"I didn't believe it," Chaddwick told me, "until once I hallucinated. I was high on acid and a friend pulled out some heroin. Right out of the box, I saw a long red acrylic nail-tipped finger emerge and point at me. I heard a female voice inside the box say, 'I want you. Come with me.'"

That was it! When he came out of the delirium, he and Shantral realized the danger of drugs and their current lifestyle. They looked at each other and asked, "Where have all the flowers gone?"

Chaddwick was very much in love with Shantral and took her home to New Jersey. She must have been as dumbfounded by his parents' bucolic mansion as I was seeing Ken's old stomping grounds for the first time. She married Chaddwick and they had two beautiful daughters.

Since Shantral now had a cook, a gardener, and a housekeeper, there wasn't much for her to do. Chaddwick became something of an art luminary for his support of the arts and involvement with the cultural life of New Jersey. It all sounds ideal, but for Shantral it wasn't. In retrospect, for her, Haight-Ashbury was nothing when compared to her new life. Shantral's real tragedy began when she moved to Easy Street.

Because of his position, Chaddwick had to entertain a lot of important people. But Shantral always managed to "have something else to do" whenever he gave a cocktail or dinner party. Knowing that Shantral had few other involvements, his colleagues and neighbors were confused when she was always absent. Chaddwick and Shantral accepted no dinner invitations as a couple and seldom went out together. Word began to spread that poor Shantral "wasn't quite right."

Years later, on a snowy night, I attended a reception for Chaddwick's mother's eightieth birthday, which was held at the Arts Club in Manhattan. At one point, I needed to excuse myself. I waited and waited outside the bathroom door. Finally, thinking it must be empty, I knocked gently. The door was opened by a middle-aged woman wearing her fur coat and in tears. She tried to race past me, but I thought I recognized her.

"Shantral?" She whirled around with a frightened look on her face. "Are you all right?" I asked. When she didn't say anything, I touched her elbow and told her I had been Kenny's girlfriend. For some reason, that seemed to break the ice. She said she had to talk to me, and we made a luncheon date for the following week. She then headed for the back door of the Arts Club and walked out into the snow. Dumbfounded, I returned to my table and didn't say anything.

The following week, we met at a downtown restaurant. Shantral was expensively dressed but looked distressed and frail. It turned out that the purpose of the lunch was she wanted to tell me how lucky I was to have escaped the "horribly pretentious lifestyle" that I might have gotten myself into. I listened to her words. However, I heard more between the lines.

TECHNIQUE #30

WATCH WHAT YOU WISH FOR!

Before donning your 100 percent wool trousers and Shetland sweater to go hunting for the highborn, a word of warning. Do a little soul-searching and ask yourself questions like the following:

1. Do I really prefer listening to Puccini rather than P. Diddy?
2. Do I know (or care) who Mondrian or Renoir is?
3. Do I really want to spend my vacations touring vineyards in a town where nobody speaks a word of English?
4. Do I really want to live by all the unspoken rules on Easy Street?

She said that all these years, she'd felt like a "fish out of water," and she hated every minute of it. She feared her "fancy neighbors" would rebuff her, and as a result, she refused to socialize with them.

"I even hated running into them when I picked the girls up at school," she said.

"Did you tell Chaddwick how you felt?" I asked.

She had, and he'd begged her to let his mother "get to know her better." Shantral said, "I knew he meant, 'Let my mother teach you what's what.' And I wasn't about to let some rich bitch tell me what and what not to do."

At that instant, it all came clear to me. The high-class lifestyle intimidated poor Shantral, and instead of learning how to fit in, she rejected it all. She became a frightened bird trapped in her gilded cage.

I make no judgment on Shantral for her choice. I merely present her feelings as a caution that if the upper-class lifestyle isn't something you wish to become accustomed to, skip to the next chapter. Because here we go with more (sometimes confounding) clues to help you crack the lifestyle of the aristocratic and affluent. The list of uppers' customs goes on and on. Stay tuned for a few more short shots of majestic minutiae.

Classy and Classless Fun and Games

If you do decide to marry a classy person, you'll be stripped of a few balls. Relax, gentlemen. What I mean is that you'll have to chuck your bowling ball, your football, your basketball, your volleyball, and your baseball. There are a few balls you can hang on to, however. Your tennis ball, your squash ball, and your golf ball are fine. Come to think of it, the smaller the balls, the higher the class. No anatomical analogies intended.

Sociologists have speculated on why bowling is in the subbasement of aristocratic sports. Paul Fussell, in his hilarious analysis of class, snobbishly wrote that proletariats like bowling because they get a "nifty uniform shirt with their own name machine-embroidered in script above one pocket. Another attraction is that you don't have to strip down to play. You can be good at it and keep your prole fatty tissue decently covered."[22] Not only that, but the big payoff is that participants can smoke and drink while hurling the ball.

Moving right along. Riding horses is in, skeet shooting is in, skiing in faraway places is in, yachting is in, and above all, sailing is in—especially if you race. Yachts count as prestigious high-class toys, providing they are at least thirty-five feet long. But they fall far short of the sailboat for several reasons. With a yacht, you can be up and running by simply turning an ignition key and steering. Whereas with sailing, you must be almost "to the manner born."

There's even a hierarchy (like everything high class) of sailboats. The wooden hull is tops, and fiberglass is bottom. This is understandable because wood is a natural fiber and fiberglass is not. Also, wooden hull repairs are much more expensive than fiberglass. Of course, houseboats are the class-bottom boats. Uppers might think that people living in such a movable abode are just floating "trailer trash."

Summing it up, if you're seeking a classy mate, do not go near a bowling alley. You'll do much better lurking along the docks of yacht and sailing clubs.

Speaking of boats, thousands of love-seeking young women annually jump on a cruise ship to find their Prince. Unfortunately, the best they'll probably do is wind up in the cabin of some handsome waiter. High-class people don't take cruise ships. Nor do they go on group tours. Unless, of course, it's an art tour spon-

Technique #31
Play Their Games

Go for small ball and big boat sports. Another way to judge the class of a sport is by how much it costs. A higher-status sport requires a great deal of expensive equipment, an expensive setting, or both—like golf. The balls are small, and the course must be constantly watered, mown, and rolled with high-cost machines, by paid servants, of course.

sored by the museum or their Ivy League alma mater. Nor, gentlemen, will you find a Princess at a resort. You'll fine some great-looking young women with summer jobs, but not old-moneyed Princesses—not even nouveau riche Princesses.

Cruise ships, resorts, vacation packages—in fact, anything advertising the word *luxury* or *gourmet* is the kiss of death for classy folk. They prefer to summer at places like Cape Cod or travel to exotic faraway places that are almost impossible to find.

I Haven't Got a Thing to Wear!

When it comes to hobnobbing with the aristocratic and affluent, you might think, "But I haven't got a thing to wear." Chances are you do—but it's resting in peace in mothballs at the bottom of your closet. These many years later, I understand why Ken pulled my old woolen slacks, cotton blouse, and moth-eaten Shetland sweater out of my closet when I was to meet his mother. You see, wool and cotton are natural fabrics. They were once living, breathing parts of a plant or an animal.

Even a small percentage of polyester, Dacron, or nylon in your dress shirt might encourage uppers to glance away. Why? Well, polyester and its dull cousins, Dacron and nylon, are so uniform and, of course, less expensive. You can't spot one interesting tattered thread in these modern fabrics. My old woolen pants were full of them. You won't find one healthy trace of sheep excrement in polyester as you might have in my old Shetland sweater.

Old-moneyed people prefer natural fibers all the way. Case in point: during Caroline Kennedy's four years at Harvard, it is documented that no unnatural fiber ever went near her body. (Obviously, since this would include underwear, it must have been her roommate, her boyfriend, or some other intimate who issued the report.)

Of course, in the interest of nabbing a classy mate, you will sometimes have to break the rules. Unfortunately, 100 percent cotton panties are dreadfully unsexy. And to my knowledge, they don't make garter belts (an all-time male favorite) in cotton.

More on moneyed fabrics. No bright colors! In fact, the more faded and pastel your garments, the better. No smoothness, no shine, and definitely no glitter (which eliminates 90 percent of the modern music world's wardrobes). Women, ignore the chapter in the *Bombshell Manual* called "The Art of Sparkle, Shimmer, & Shine." Forget the bit that talks about wearing clothes that accentuate your curves. Forget risking your life tottering in impossibly high strappy sandals. Are they funky? Yes. Fun? Yes. Favorable for finding a classy guy? No! You'll do better meeting the family in flat brown Birkenstocks.

"Oh, how tediously these high-class people dress," you must be saying to yourself. Sadly, it's a fact. They don't wish to advertise sensuality to any peasant who happens to glance their way.

But not to worry, sisters. You can still be an "inner bombshell." You can be secretly sexy, whimsical, feminine, capricious, sentimental, and dynamite—in bed.

Likewise, not to worry, gentlemen. You needn't shed your raw masculine stud-hunk qualities. In fact, every woman wants a man who has rock-hard desire for her 'round the clock. A classy woman just wants it to be her delicious secret. Well, maybe she'll gleefully whisper about your prowess to her best friend—whose blue blood will turn green with envy.

For the moment, think wooly, textured, nubby, and, weather permitting, definitely layered. Gentlemen, you're "in" when you stroll through the doorway of a party in a tweed jacket with a Shetland crew-neck pullover. If your Oxford cloth shirt is just peeping over the top and you're sporting a long wool scarf, you're sure to catch the eye of every classy lady in the room. This is a bit of a challenge in Florida and Southern California, to be sure.

Nevertheless, when hunting high-class quarry, go as close to the Northeastern country leisure look as you can get.

Scruffy Beats Spotless

Now, one would assume that wearing neat, clean, new clothes would also be a turn-on to a classy person. Wrong! You see, doing so might indicate that your social circumstances are not entirely secure and you need to prove that you can afford the newest duds and endless dry cleaning. Royals often consciously sport old clothes. Sometimes it's as though they're trying to prove how much conventional dignity they can afford to discard.

I had always admired impeccable cleanliness. I once dated a self-proclaimed social climber. If at dinner one little drop of oil fell to his trousers, no spot remover would suffice. The droplet could be practically undetectable to the naked eye, but he'd race off to the cleaners with those pants. The very rich assiduously avoiding pretension crowd would ask, "Who's he trying to impress?"

Best Hunting Duds in the Old-Moneyed Crowd

Let's say you're going classy-mate hunting at a party. Gentlemen, if your overcoat is navy blue, olive, or any color but beige, take it off before you make your grand entrance. If it's black, roll it in a ball and hide it in the hallway. In fact, if you should be so lucky as to have a classy lady on your arm as you depart, leave your black raincoat in the corner for the janitor to find. He'll appreciate the fitting addition to his wardrobe. If you're in doubt about the type of coat to wear, your Brooks Brothers or Burberry salesman will gladly help you choose an acceptably expensive beige one.

Women, fur is fine for the non–animal-rights crowd. For younger, more socially conscious Royals, cream-colored camel hair is the coat of choice. The women's department of Brooks Brothers or Burberry can help you.

One of the most crucial aspects of classy attire is that it fit perfectly. Women, that means no skirts too large around the waist or too tight around the buns. (Sorry, bombshells.) Gentlemen, that means not being able to place even a baby finger between the back of your neck and your jacket.

For leisure wear, both men and women can use a Chris-Craft mail-order catalog as a style guide. Windbreakers with lots of drawstrings and topsider shoes (for gripping the deck of your sailboat, of course) with no socks are appropriate. Clothing with buoys, lobsters, signal flags, or anything else whispering "I've just stepped off my yacht" will suffice.

When it comes to bathing attire, think modest, think boring, think *un*sexy. Men, that means boxer trunks for you at the beach. Women, that means one-piece swimsuits with tiny skirts attached. Ho-hum.

TECHNIQUE #32
DRESS DULL

One hundred percent cotton is in. One hundred percent wool is in. One hundred percent silk is in. Fur and leather or anything that was once alive is one hundred percent in. In the old-moneyed crowd, your status is inversely proportional to the number of polyester threads in your clothing. The name of the classy garb game is nothing man-made and nothing shiny, spotless, or too colorful.

Women, needless to say, discard your capri pants. If they are purple or have any patterns or shine to the material, incinerate them. Sorry, no leather skirts. Uppers have only a half dozen acceptable uses of leather, such as for shoes, belts, handbags, gloves, camera cases, and dog leashes. (There are, perhaps, a few other X-rated uses for leather accoutrements, but that's always behind closed doors and not to be introduced until you're well into a relationship.)

Wallets, too, can be leather. But not bulging with credit cards, photos, or nostalgic ticket stubs or overflowing with hundred-dollar bills, mafia style. The smaller the wallet, the more tasteful.

The business apparel of choice for both classy Princes and Princesses is suits. Suits are also perfectly acceptable attire when you go to a cocktail party during the week. In fact, Jackie Kennedy would go right from her publishing office to a soiree dressed in a suit. Suits should be plain with no fancy buttons, no belts in the back of the jacket, no ornamentation, no nothing. Just a tiny designer label sewn tastefully inside. Women, you can dress up your plain suit with a fancier blouse, but only in silk, lace, or cotton, of course.

Jewelry? Gentlemen, forget anything but a watch. Women, you're fine with gold and real gems—but very few.

Aspiring uppers, let's talk about your watch. Your watch receives Royal points indirectly proportional to the number of features it has. Starting with 10 points, subtract points for each of the following:

It's digital—Subtract 8
It displays the time in Paris, London, Rome, or Kuala
    Lumpur—Subtract 5
It has the number of days elapsed in the year—Subtract 4
It has a second hand—Subtract 1 (the leisure class doesn't
    need to track seconds)

The classy watch of preference for both men and women is the Cartier tank watch with a black lizard strap. Before we leave the wrist area, gentlemen, you might think cuff links are classy. Nevertheless, an upper would dismiss them as pretentious.

Working your way down your body, you must absolutely not have a pocket protector for pens. That would signal how often you reach for your pen to hastily note whatever your boss orders you to do. Above all, have nothing hanging from your belt. That includes cell phones, sunglass cases, and, unspeakably, keys.

Now moving back up, I want to address the constant quandary of the necktie—to wear or not to wear. Going with no necktie signals "I'm above it all" and "I don't need to impress anyone." However, in today's business society, going to an appointment without a tie is tantamount to going in your jockey shorts. The guideline to use on your tie is that there must be nothing self-congratulatory or even self-revealing about it. For example, tiny yachts or signal flags on your necktie flaunt "I own a yacht. Me rich." Flying pheasants brag "I'm a sport. Me cool." Little trombones: "I'm a musician. Me artistic." Little scales: "I'm an attorney. Me professional." Little dolphins: "I'm a nature lover. Me fine person."

No, the most acceptable classy tie has small white dots against a dark background. (Don't worry—this does not signify "Me spotty.") The fashion statement here is that there is none. It is evidence that you are not trying to identify with anything.

DRESSING CASUALLY FOR THE QUALITY QUARRY KILL

Above all, any clothes with visible writing on them are off-limits. Even the designer's name, no matter how tastefully small or woven into initials, is classless if legible.

You may remember I mentioned my cherished and comfy Coca-Cola T-shirt with "It's the real thing!" written on it. Oh, how I loved that red T-shirt! I'd had it for a long time, and it had the original Coca-Cola emblem in lovely white cursive letters plastered across the front.

Imagine my despair when I discovered it would occasion a stately snort. You will not find one article of clothing with writing on it in high-class closets. This includes caps with messages on them and practically all popular T-shirts—some of which can be pretty pitiful. Many of them broadcast the wearer's warped sense of humor, attitudes, bad habits, frail ego, or sexual perversions.

I understand why such shirts would turn off a Royal soul, but I used to think some of my own T-shirts were pretty cool. I relished wearing my *Redbook*, *Cosmopolitan*, and even *Penthouse* T-shirts when I wrote for those magazines. I felt real upscale around the neighborhood when I sported my Barnes & Noble or my New York City Ballet tees. I surmised that my Beethoven shirt would assure any passing Prince that I was a connoisseur of classical music.

Sadly, after learning about the lifestyles of high-class people, I now realize that these full-frontal ads were obviously misguided attempts to show how well read, cultural, or limber I was.

THE FASHION KISS OF DEATH

Now we come to the fashion kiss of death for capturing a high-class mate. Unfortunately for some men, it's more fathomable to step outside their front door without their trousers than without the omnipresent baseball cap proclaiming their affiliation to a favorite sports team or beer of choice. It gets worse. If you want to make absolutely sure a classy lady won't even look your way, no matter how handsome your face under it, spin your baseball cap and display the one-size-fits-all adjustable strap in the front.

Once a girlfriend and I were having lunch in a sports bar. A guy in a backward-facing baseball cap, clutching a bottle of beer, came staggering over to our table. My friend successfully blew him off and then rolled her eyes. I asked her a question that had baffled me for years: "Why does he turn his baseball cap around?"

She answered, as if the explanation were as obvious and tasteless as a rat turd in a sugar bowl, "It's to keep the sun off his red neck." Rednecks are not at the top of a Princess's most-wanted man-in-my-life list.

Further evidence of the baseball cap blacklisting you is that you search in vain trying to find one in any all-class mail-order catalog. Even the upper-middle-class L. L. Bean catalog draws the line at baseball caps. The catalog offers men a variety of headgear like straw hats, bucket hats, mountain walker hats, fur felt outdoorsman hats, cotton bucket hats, and sou'wester rain hats, but nary a baseball cap is buried in its pages. If you want to signal to a highborn Royal that you're one, too, then burn your baseball cap.

And regarding the rest of your body, beware of even the tiniest self-advertisements, such as college rings, gold-plated blazer buttons with university seals, and Phi Beta Kappa keys, each of which tell a Royal, "I have something to prove."

However, do not go pitching half your wardrobe into the reject pile as I was recently tempted to do. Remember, you must stick to all this pretentious-sounding stuff only if you're out to capture big-time Royalty. Secretly, your *Atlantic Monthly* T-shirt or *New York Review of Books* jacket would impress me. But don't tell anybody.

HATS AND HAIR THAT SCORE WITH HIGH-CLASS PEOPLE

Obviously, punk Mohawks, rattails, hair extensions, funky dreadlocks (unless you're rich and famous), pixie bangs, the spiky look, flapper bobs, chili bowl, poodle, or duck's ass haircuts, or colors that don't appear anywhere in nature are not high on the list of acceptable classy hairstyles. Neither is the restrictive every-hair-in-its-place style where each strand looks like it has been perfectly and strategically placed, then sprayed or glued to your head.

Actually, women, you have greater leeway in acceptable hairstyles. If you choose short hair, break the bank for a good cut. You don't need to go to one of those expensive pretentious shops where you pay by the follicle. But if you do want short hair, make it look expensive. Then avoid any obvious hair spray.

Don't worry if you're lazy in the hair department. Most upperclass men admire a soft medium-length hairstyle or even a ponytail. Natural healthy shine is the name of the mane game. In fact, you'll probably be right in fashion if you wear the same style you did years ago. (Unless, that is, you were a forerunner of the multicolored finger-in-an-electric-socket punk look.) Take a nostalgic look back at your high school or college yearbook. Many upperclass women keep their hair for a lifetime the same way they did at boarding school.

Gentlemen, what's the best woman-pleasing style? Out of 10 women, 9.9 preferred a style that was professional, neat, clean, and not styled, dyed, or sprayed. Such a cut says you're not too vain, cheap, or concerned with any one group's opinion of you. It merely signals, "I'm successful and I take some care with my grooming."

No matter what your age, go to a talented traditional hairdresser who has that knack for knowing which style goes with your face. Gentlemen, do not try to camouflage any spots on your head that are less thickly populated than you like. Above all, do not salvage a few long hairs to comb over the top of your head. She will see your chrome dome shining through, and it's total humiliation on windy days. Princess-worthy men are secure enough that they don't need to pretend they have more money, more prestige, or more hair than they actually do.

The Most Accurate Class Indicator

No matter how you dress, how you wear your hair, or how you furnish your home, the moment you open your mouth, your social class will show.

In the seventeenth century, Ben Jonson gave us wisdom for the ages. He said, "Language most shows a man. Speak, that I may see thee." Refined people are extremely sensitive to the words you choose and the way you pronounce them. Unfortunately, one verbal slip could fracture a relationship with an upper, and you'd never know the reason.

Let's say you are at a singles party and you meet an attractive man or woman who in conversation happens to say, "Him and me ain't gonna." Your interest would probably crack like a walnut shell. Before the sentence is finished, you've speculated that the speaker's educational level is a notch or two or three below yours.

Likewise, you get about seven seconds when you meet someone to prove whether you're permanent mate material or not. Well-educated ears are fine-tuned to pick up subtle mistakes. They are sensitive to subtleties that seem perfectly OK to most people.

Even using the wrong pronoun could knock you out of the Royal ring. You could suffer a KO if you say, "Him and me went," instead of, "He and I went." Or, "He gave it to you and I," instead of, "He gave it to you and me."

High on the list of uppers' verbal sins are bloopers like, "I couldn't hardly do it" or "He don't want it" or "Irregardless of the situation."

Even tiny mistakes loom large in their ears. "Where is he at?" is not a horrible grammatical mistake. It wouldn't signal that you're a lowlife. But it could definitely scratch you off an upper's poten-

> ### Technique #33
> ## Listen to the Sweet Sound of Class
>
> Spin your radio dial beyond the acid rock, heavy metal,
> country music, inspirational, pop, rap, golden oldie,
> and even news stations. Keep your dial on the local
> classical music station, and let your ears do the rest.
> Most classical music stations have polished and cultured
> announcers. Listening half an hour each day will inject
> your veins with sufficient blue blood to hold your own
> in any Royal crowd.

tial partner list. Grammar is a great linguistic divide between the
classes.

Now, here's where it gets really tricky. Even if your grammar
is impeccable, your choice of words could mess you up. Would
you believe you could say something that sounds perfectly acceptable to most of us, like, "They are very affluent and have a lovely
home," and it might mean curtains with an upper-class prospect?

Why? Because of the substitution of "affluent" for "rich."
Royalty consider that a middle-class pretentious affectation. The
uppers shun words like *wealthy* or *affluent*. They say, "rich" (like
they are!), plain and simple.

To continue, why not say, "home"? Because that's a much too
commercial real-estate word. The rich don't live in homes. They
live in (and speak of) houses. Would you believe that calling the
facilities the "little girls' room" or "little boys' room" could be the
overture to your swan song with an upper. Call it like it is, they
say. It's a toilet!

Class-watcher Paul Fussell warns of other middle-class word traps, such as *individuals, purchase, launder, currently, proceed, request, subsequently, terminate, utilize, cocktails, correctional facility, previous, vocalist, passed away,* and *gratuity*.

What's wrong with using those words? Again, they are rife with pretension. Uppers just say *people, buy, wash, go, later, end, use, drinks, jail, before, singer, died,* and *tip*. What does an upper need to prove to anybody, and why would they even try?

The lower you go, the worse it gets. Uppers say, "She is pregnant"; middles say, "She is expecting"; and lowers say, "She's in a family way." Stick with the simple. The fewer syllables, the better. But don't mispronounce it! It's painful to an upper's ears to hear you say "fack" instead of "fact" or "roasbeef" instead of "roast beef." Oh, and be sure to finish saying all words ending with g. "Goin'," "bein'," and "havin'" are the most common proletariat betrayal words.

Now add to this the further complication of volume. In a restaurant or any other public place, you'll never overhear uppers chatting at the next table. They speak much more softly than those lower on the ladder, who often turn up the volume on voices—and their radios. Uppers don't need to impose their presence on everyone within earshot.

The list of linguistic boners and foot-in-mouth possibilities is almost endless. So what's the solution? Back to "location, location, location." Hang around a classy neighborhood enough and you'll start to speak like them.

Can't move? Then turn the radio to a high-class station (better than TV) so you won't be tempted to let your eyes interfere with your ears.

You could write an encyclopedia on the list of noble no-nos. It seems that even traditions that sound refined to the untutored have an underlying message that your high-class potential mate would view condescendingly.

For instance, discard the custom of writing a once-a-year Christmas or Hanukkah letter filling in extended family and friends on the last year's personal news. At best, a true upper would view such a letter as flaunting your recent triumphs, thus again trying to prove something.

The all-American scorn for the "good fences make good neighbors" sentiment is missing in the upper class. Dropping in for a visit without phoning first is a deplorable transgression. Even close family members living in the same countryside wouldn't dream of it.

The list goes on. Perhaps now you'll understand my location, location, location recommendation more clearly. It's virtually impossible to pick up on these and the hundreds of other subtleties that gush through blue blood. You can, however, absorb them all by osmosis when sharing a zip code.

How Important Are Looks to Classy People?

The answer? Your appearance is just as important to upper-class lovers as to any Hunter or Huntress of love. That means the face card counts, a lot—maybe even more. Princes and paupers alike go for attractive women. Likewise, a man's looks are important to a woman whether she's a Princess or a prostitute.

But here's the rub. What uppers consider good looking is a tad different from those on the lower rungs of life's ladder. A study called "Female Preferences for Male Physiques" disclosed women's preferences in a man's physical characteristics from the length of his toes to the length of other more interesting bodily parts.[23]

Here's the bottom line. Gentlemen, if you are pursuing an upper-class woman, you're in luck if you are tall and slim and have a sensitive, intelligent face. She'll go for a slender body over beef-cake every time.

Conversely, the study indicated that women who were lower on the food chain of society, such as women in menial jobs, were wild about hefty, hunky muscle men. Higher-class women choose men who have a longer neck, as this is a perceived characteristic of aristocracy.

Both men and women have a much better shot at uppers if they are thin. For some reason, obesity and blue blood don't mix. Being heavy subconsciously signals to uppers that perhaps you're on a diet of fast food and beer or you're a victim of nervous overeating. They might surmise that you're a sucker for McDonald's TV ads that encourage going out for breakfast to chow down on an Egg McMuffin or two.

A mere century ago, corpulence paralleled success. But that is no longer the case. Obviously the upper classes have enough to eat. Yet your thin body suggests you've also been successful in the most important slenderizing exercise—pushing yourself away from the table. In fact, obesity is four times more prevalent in the lower middle class than it is among those higher on the class totem pole. British writer Jonathan Raban found American social mores fascinating. Offensively, he carried around a mental tape measure at a Minnesota state fair. He calculated middle-class waistlines as people walked by, enjoying their hot dogs and sugar cones. He cruelly maligned the unsuspecting chubbies.

Mr. Raban wrote, "These farming families . . . are descendants of hungry immigrants from Germany and Scandinavia. Generation by generation, their families have eaten themselves into Americans. Now they all have the same figure: same broad bottom, same Buddha belly, same neckless join between a turkey-waddle chin and a sperm-whale torso. The women poured themselves into pink elasticized pantsuits; the men swelled against every seam and button of their plaid shirts and Dacron slacks." (Whew, if that isn't enough to make you push your plate away, I don't know what is.)

Rabin perversely went so far as to create a "Fatness Map." His bizarre project suggested that the most obese Americans live in areas of the most recent immigration, where ancestral memories of hunger are the closest. The skinniest folks live in states settled by pioneers before 1776. If your ancestors came over on the *Mayflower*, you are most likely slender. Rabin decreed that the flab capital of the country is somewhere in the Minnesota-Iowa-Dakotas triangle.

I don't think Mr. Rabin wins the Politically Correct Award of the Year. Nevertheless, his outlandish research offers one explanation of why thin is in with aristocrats.

Technique #34
Diet and Dress to Disguise "Deficiencies"

Now for the good news about all this snobbish stuff about looks. Let good clothing and good carriage camouflage any ways that God shortchanged you in the looks department. Stand and move like an upper. They hold their hands close to their bodies when they walk and have more controlled and precise movements. Serfs swing their arms and amble along more flat-footedly. Nobility stand tall. Nonnoble nobodies might slouch as if to say, "Whip me again, Master."

Now Are You Sure You Want It?

If after hearing about all the minutiae that come between "How do you do" and "Good-bye" you still want the high-class lifestyle, go for it! Just remember, the "rules" are unspoken and unyielding. The exclusion is subtle and the rewards are uncertain. But if "high" is the class you aspire to, reread this chapter. It will help turn your blood blue.

How to Find an Honorable Mate

Where Have All the Good Men and Women Gone?

OK, OK. You know you're sick of all the croaking frogs around you, even the great-looking rich ones. You're searching for one good man or woman. You want your lifetime partner to be a "good person," one who doesn't lie, steal, or cheat on you.

In a word, what one quality do all good people have? See if you can guess. It begins with an *i* (as in I, me, myself). It ends with a *y* (as in you). It includes the word *grit* (like backbone, courage, character, decency, honesty, honor, and principles).

The key word is—drumroll, please—*integrity*. It is the sine qua non of captivating then capturing a good person.

First, you have to define integrity. This alone is not a piece of cake. Throughout the ages, wise men and women have laid their eggheads on their pillows and spent sleepless nights pondering this essential element. Philosophers, sages, attorneys, debate-team students, politicians (well, some of the latter), and just plain folks have discussed and debated integrity—who has it and who doesn't. Everyone's definition is different.

To come up with a workable definition of integrity, I probed everywhere—dictionaries, encyclopedias, the Web, all my friends, and even a few drunks at a local bar. Synonyms and definitions that almost always popped up were "honesty," "sincerity," "having sound moral principles," "being trustworthy," "caring about others," "self-knowledge," and so forth. There were a multitude of definitions, but practically everyone I asked included "telling the truth" as at least part of the definition. They all agreed that truth was integral to integrity.

But being 100 percent truthful is not that easy. The big question is when is something a little white lie, and when is it a big whopper? The answer is if what comes out of your mouth is 100 percent to save someone else's feelings or ego—if it truly is only for them and involves something minor—the lie might be excusable. Underscore that *might*. You should try to avoid lying at all costs. Not only because you are committed to capturing a high-quality mate, but because you might get caught and lose their respect forever.

A girlfriend asked me to go shopping with her after work on a Monday evening. Sheila and I had gone on a previous shopping excursion, and she had been as slow and annoying as a dripping faucet. She tried on every skirt in the shop. Then, gawking at her own rear end in the mirror, she'd interrogate me. "Does this make me look fat?" (All the skirts did, and I was getting ticked at the dozens of times I had to dish out a white lie.) So this time when she asked me to go shopping with her, I declined, saying that I had a previous engagement.

It didn't do much for our friendship when I (shopping alone) ran into her that Monday evening at the makeup counter at Macy's. A little white lie gone awry. Even when an untruth is trivial and you call it "a white lie," you must reclassify it as a "mini-whopper" if it's self-serving. If you get caught in just one of those, you can lose your honorable potential partner. Part of your arsenal of weapons to capture principled prey is to always tell the truth.

I know I lost the trust of a high-quality potential partner one time when I told a self-serving fib. It was a day when I had to leave for the airport at four in the afternoon. I desperately wanted to talk to my then boyfriend, a very moral man. Just before leaving, I called him. I got his answering machine and left him a message saying, "Please call me soon because I'm leaving for the airport at three."

At 3:45 the phone rang. I answered it and heard the voice of my very surprised soon-to-be-ex boyfriend. I knew at that moment his respect for me started to crumble. I resolved after that to stamp out even microscopically small white lies forever if they have a selfish motive.

Have you ever been in an antique store and you see a beautiful bowl or teacup you really want to buy? You pick it up and turn it around and around in your hands inspecting it. Looks pretty good. But then you find one tiny hairline crack. You'd probably be disappointed and sadly place it back on the shelf. It's the same with your integrity when dealing with a principled potential partner. If you have one tiny crack in your teacup, you become damaged property in the eyes of an honorable person.

When you have integrity, it's like wearing a suit of armor. The truth will make you invulnerable. Living with integrity is like living in a strong house that no big bad wolf can blow down. I'm sure you've heard the story that begins "Once upon a time there were three little pigs. . . ."

> The three little pigs all went out from their mommy's mud hole one day to make their way in the world and they all built houses. The first little

pig built his of straw, the second one constructed his out of sticks, and the third of bricks.

One day the big bad wolf came and knocked on the first little pig's door and said, "Little pig, little pig, let me come in." And the little pig answered, "No, no, I won't let you come in, not by the hair on my chinny chin chin." "Well," said the wolf, "then I'll huff and I'll puff and I'll blow your house in." So he huffed and he puffed and he blew the house in and then ate the poor little pig.

The second little pig met the same sad fate, also becoming tasty pork tartare for the wolf, because his house was only made of sticks.

♡ Technique #35
You Lie? You Lose

Never let the smallest lie creep into your communication with a moral person because if you get caught even once in a lie, in a self-serving exaggeration, or being less than forthright, your believability starts to go out the door. And you risk your future mate soon following.

When my mother told me this bedtime story, I'm sure she didn't suspect that the distressing tale scared me to death. After she turned out the lights, I'd quiver under my covers, petrified that the big bad wolf would come gobble me up.

But the story has a happy ending—not to mention a moral.

> The third and wisest little pig built his house with bricks. And sure enough, the wolf came and knocked at his door, all confident and licking his chops. He used his standard line, "Little pig, little pig, let me come in," to which the little pig responded, "No, no, I won't let you in, not by the hair on my chinny chin chin."
>
> "Well," said the wolf, "then I'll huff and I'll puff and I'll blow your house in." So he huffed and he puffed, and he puffed and he huffed, and he huffed and he puffed. But this time he couldn't blow the little pig's house in. It was solid because it was built of bricks. So sure of the brick house he had built, the little pig just went waddling happily around his kitchen, unfazed by the threatening force outside.

When I was a little girl, my mother would often come to my room, knock on the door, and in a mock threatening voice say, "Leilie, if your room is a mess, I'll huff and I'll puff and I'll blow your room in." I would answer, "No, no, you won't, not by the hair on my chinny chin chin." (And then, of course, I would clean it up on the double.)

Other times, if my mother discovered I'd told a little white lie, she'd sternly say, "I'll huff and I'll puff and I'll blow that lie in." That, of course, was my cue to say, "No, no, you won't, not by the hair on my chinny chin chin." And then I'd confess. Why?

Because saying "not by the hair on my chinny chin chin" made me remember with horror the fate of the first two little pigs, whose houses were weak. Only the little pig with a strong house survived. Uttering "chinny chin chin" prompted me to make sure my story was as solid as bricks.

Technique #36
Build Your Beliefs in Brick

When you build a solid brick structure of your beliefs, principles, and integrity, you become invulnerable to all attacks. And only when your beliefs and principles are of equally high quality can you expect to capture an honorable person.

No Slipups in Your Scruples Diet

To be worthy of an honorable person, you have to live honorably—all the time and with everyone in your life. Even deceased diet doctor Robert Atkins lets you sneak an occasional candy bar. But integrity is different. One slipup with your principled potential mate, and you're history. But shaping up overnight is difficult, and we're bound to slip up at first.

So what do you do if you find yourself in the unfortunate situation where he or she catches you in a character clunker, like taking towels from a hotel or not speaking up when the cashier gives you too much change? You must make amends—fast. Letting an honorable person know that your conscience pangs are killing you isn't enough. You've got to rack your poor moral brain with ways to make up for your mistake to retain an honorable person's respect.

Coming Clean Counts

Once, many years ago, I had a little theater project. My theatrical partner and I had an off-off-Broadway show on weekends. We performed in what we called *The Project*. Every Friday and Saturday night, we did scenes from scripts we'd written during the week. Since our scenes always had a message (and sometimes a bunch of entertaining baloney), we developed a good following.

The only other person involved in our little presentation was a woman named Donna. She did everything—took reservations, set the props, sold tickets at the door, and even helped us clean up after the show. I once asked Donna why she did all this for so little money. She laughed and said she was like the circus janitor who, while he was shoveling up elephant dung, was asked why he kept such a dirty job. He responded, "I just love show business." Well, Donna loved show business (or at least our feeble attempt at it), and we loved Donna.

The show, because it was held at my loft, went on every weekend for several years. After the show's run, as they like to say in show business, we lost track of Donna. And Father Time, as he usually does, clouds memory. I'd almost forgotten about my faithful friend Donna.

Then one day, about three years later, I opened my mailbox and found a bulging envelope with no return address on it. I opened it. Money came tumbling out as if three bars had appeared in a row on a Las Vegas slot machine. It was a jackpot of seven hundred dollars and thirty-two cents, to be precise—and nothing else. I dove back into the envelope to find an explanation. There stuck to the side was a hand-scrawled note on a Post-it:

"Here is the money I stole from the box office receipts at *The Project*. I'm sorry. Donna." I turned the Post-it over, but there was no phone number, no return address, nothing.

A sea of memories engulfed me, and I felt a wave of sympathy for Donna. Not because she'd been a petty thief. But because of the torture her conscience must have given her over the years.

Within the hour, however, my sympathy had turned to respect. To this day, I wish I could find Donna to express my admiration for her confession and making restitution. But I've forgotten her last name. (Donna, if you're reading this, please contact me!)

Recently, I've had another emotion on this. Now I feel a flood of joy for Donna, because wherever she is, she surely has self-respect. Self-respect always translates into confidence and high self-esteem. And these are the qualities that you must have to capture a high-quality mate.

TECHNIQUE #37
YOU MESS UP? YOU MAKE IT UP

If you blew it and get caught having done something less than honorable, you must make amends—fast! It may seem forced after the fact, but your Royal will respect you for it. And your being honorable is more important to Royalty than your momentarily looking foolish.

Why Does This Need for Similarity Run So Deep?

When you are seeking a good person, that's where "You gotta be one to get one" is especially true. A group of love researchers had a field day observing, investigating, analyzing, and categorizing who marries whom. Synthesizing all the studies, the big headline is that people generally marry someone who is similar to them in the deeper things in life.

Why does your honorable Royal want someone similar? You'd think that someone who was different might be unpredictable and thus exciting. A *dissimilar other*, as the studies like to call it, could provide new information, new insights, and an interesting way of looking at life. These sound like enticements, don't they?

Unfortunately, it doesn't work that way. No matter how unique, wonderful, and different you may be, if you're not 100 percent ethical, you lose. Chances are your desired Royal will choose someone equally royal in thought and action to be his or her permanent mate. Your desired mate may date someone in a lower league for a while, but when it comes to permanence, honorables want a partner who shares comparable beliefs and values in life. They want a mate who has a similar way of viewing the world and their reason for being in it. And, of course, an ethical person wants someone with matching integrity.

All the research into this fascinating sociological verity backs it up. In one typical study, students, before moving into a dormitory where researchers knew they'd eventually be getting to know each other pretty well, were given a survey.[24] To determine the students' beliefs and values, the researchers asked them how they felt about some of the more important things in life. The researchers' hypothesis was that as the students became better acquainted with each other, they would gravitate to the others who held similar views. The researchers predicted which ones would become friends or couples.

Sure enough, the sociologists were right on target! People with similar views wound up as friends or as lovers.

Sadly, many frogs never know why they are exiled by their Prince or Princess. It's tough to say to someone, "I'm breaking up with you because you're not a good enough person."

Why do ethical people only want someone with high morals? One, because life is scary—yes, even to Princes and Princesses. And people feel a lot safer and happier around someone who is similar. The reasons are many. Every time you agree with someone, your beliefs are reinforced. Your agreement serves as independent evidence that your opinions, interests, and values are correct.

This is particularly rewarding for highly ethical people who perhaps have been knocking their heads against the corporate world. They have probably encountered principles and values that went against their ethical grain. Then when you come along in complete accord with their values, it's especially rewarding.

Beware of agreeing with everything they say, however. You don't want to sound like a yes-person. A study called "A Reinforcement-Affect Model of Attraction" demonstrated that it was not the number of small agreements but the proportion of agreement on the more weighty matters in life that caused "coupling."

Character Counts

Many people who think they've found their lifetime partner get an unhappy surprise. They think everything is going great. Then powie!—right in the kisser. He or she tells you that you are history. Has it ever happened to you? You happily thought you'd found your dream partner, but he or she suddenly breaks up with you? And you don't have a clue why. You lie awake at night with your head on a tear-soaked pillow. You go over every action and word the two of you exchanged in the last days of the love affair. And you still can't figure it out.

Men have a special challenge in the honor department because if signals of a guy's shabby integrity start to flash at an ethical woman, she'll give the optimistic boyfriend his walking papers—pronto, without an explanation. The poor bloke is left scratching his head during his forced retreat.

When he asks her, "What went wrong?" she usually doesn't tell him because she doesn't want to hurt his feelings. It's a rare woman who will say, "I'm breaking up with you because your principles don't live up to my standards."

We women are on the lookout for your character right up front. (For men, that concern traditionally comes a tad later.) Gentlemen, you could be good looking and have a great job, a decent amount of money, and a winning personality. You're about to pop the question to your Princess when, out of the blue, she tells you it's all over. As you desperately scramble to pick up the pieces of your smashed-to-smithereens heart, you ask yourself over and over, "What happened?"

You may never know it, but if she is an honorable woman, there is a good chance it's your principles that did you in. If you were not raised in a household where the highest moral standards were the norm, and absolute truth and honesty were taken for granted, your ethical standards, although high, might not have reached the pinnacle of hers.

Gentlemen, be aware, from the moment you meet a woman, that she is on the lookout for emblems of your beliefs, your values, your principles, your character. One lie, one ill remark, one cheapness of attitude on a first date with her can mean you'll never have a second.

I once liked a man so much—in fact, I was in love with him—that, although I discovered his values were very different from mine, I initially thought they were similar. I certainly don't intend to cast myself in the role of "Princess" here, but in relation to him, I thought I was pretty royal. The gentleman I'm talking about proved himself to be a frog in a Prince's disguise.

The Prince Who Turned Out to Be a Frog

The man I loved was a Canadian named Ryan. Ryan was tall, good looking, clever, a fabulous dresser, and very exciting in the erotic and romance departments. He had an electrifying cache of mystery about him. To top it off, Ryan was eleven years younger, which fed my ego tremendously. One night Ryan concealed a beautiful diamond engagement ring in a dozen roses he gave me. In spite of our age difference, I was tempted to think of him as a permanent partner.

I believed he was a man of high standards. Ryan was a faithful churchgoer and spoke often of his spirituality. Many of his stories underscored his commitment to truth and his honesty. He seemed ideal.

Until one or two trivial matters sent up a tiny red flag. First, his telephone. Ryan had caller ID blocked on his phone so I couldn't read his number when he called me. That in itself would have been nothing. But since I didn't have the caller ID blocked feature on my phone, my number always showed up on his phone whenever I called him. Knowing who was calling, Ryan would answer with, "Hi, Leil," "Hello, sweetheart," or something similar.

But on the few occasions when I called him from a pay phone whose number he didn't recognize on his caller ID, he didn't even say hello until I spoke. In other words, any caller would have to identify him- or herself before Ryan would say his name or even utter a sound. Hmm.

Furthermore, whenever we were in his apartment and his phone rang, I noticed he would carefully scrutinize the caller ID box before picking up the receiver. If he didn't recognize the number, he'd let the phone company's generic message answer. It was obvious that Ryan wasn't identifying himself until he knew who was on the other end of the line. Who was he avoiding?

Once I jokingly questioned him about it. Ryan quickly explained that it was because he didn't welcome unsolicited sales calls. In retrospect, when I think about it, avoiding sales calls didn't warrant that much evasive action. But because I was infatuated with him, I accepted his answer.

I closed my eyes to other small indications. We once traveled to Bermuda together, and he seemed very nervous when we went through immigrations. I often do consulting work on the island, and a few of the officers recognize me. When we got to the immigrations booth, Ryan asked me to go through first and requested that I say casually to the officer, "My fiancé is next." When I asked why, he replied, "Because you are so beautiful and I'm proud that you're my woman." My infatuation and freshly fed ego made me accept that answer, too. It didn't cross my mind that he might have other reasons to fear immigrations folk.

His passion for me and for his spirituality was stealing my heart. Like immersing myself in a warm bubble bath, I was tempted to plunge into the relationship. I was almost ready to submerge myself and say yes to a life with him when a few more drops of doubt began to spill over onto the floor.

He wanted to introduce me to his family. During the visit, his sister told me she was so happy that Ryan was in touch again because there had been "a period of several years when nobody knew where he was." When questioned, Ryan said that he had "had a falling out" with his dad and, as a result, he hadn't let the family know where he was. I didn't like that. My blinders were starting to slip.

Then came the final blow. Soon after our visit, I was fixing dinner at my apartment for Ryan, who was coming at seven. Out my kitchen window, I saw a burglar furtively climbing the fire escape across the street. I called 911. Just as I hung up, Ryan arrived. I pulled him over to the window and pointed out the thief who, by now, was trying to lift the neighbor's window. When I told Ryan I'd called 911 and the police were on the way over, he went ballistic and shouted at me that he didn't like "snooping cops."

Ryan's car left rubber on the road as he peeled out of my driveway. I'd already set the table with candles, and a Cornish hen was roasting in the oven. I was hurt and confused. Then, in my wounded state, I started piecing together other of Ryan's actions that, at the time, had seemed perfectly innocent. For example, whenever he got in his car, he would assiduously turn on the radar detector. He even attached it in my car when we rode in it. Retrospectively, it was evident that Ryan definitely wanted to avoid law enforcement officers. The evidence was mounting that he was hiding something. I told him of my suspicions.

Technique #38
Take an Integrity X-Ray

Schedule a summit conference with the person you've lived with since the day you were born—yourself. You know that individual pretty well. Make a list of where you are strong in the character department and where you fall short. Then resolve to work on the latter. I know this is not your average advice on how to captivate a man or woman. But if you're after an honorable person, it's critical.

At that, my beloved Dr. Jekyll suddenly turned into a vitriolic and sardonic Mr. Hyde. As his tires screeched out of my driveway the final time, I let out a sigh of relief—and a bucket of tears. And then I cried another bucket for him because, poor guy, he never knew what was coming. I must have seemed like a totally irrational woman who suddenly broke up with him for no good reason.

Why have I told you this story? The message is that if I (who pride myself on open communicating) didn't even tell Ryan about my major confusions and disappointments, how can you expect your lost love to tell you of his or her reason for breaking it off? Unfortunately, if you have any qualities that an honorable person could interpret as character flaws, the ax will probably come unexpectedly. That's just the way people are.

The solution? Just as you would examine your body for any blotches after a walk through poison ivy, examine your personality for any spots that might turn your Royal off. And then either eradicate those flaws or explain them early in the relationship.

Incidentally, I eventually discovered that Ryan did have a checkered past and a few entanglements with the law. How naive I was! We women especially put on blinders to any negative qualities in a man we love. For a while, that is.

Come Across as a "Really Good Person" from the Get-Go

It is crucial to display Royal qualities immediately because a fascinating phenomenon factors into this. That is, if you get a "clean bill of character" on the first few dates and a Royal starts to like you, he or she is apt to overlook telltale signals of less-than-optimum qualities later on. Why? Because people who like someone's personality are more apt to assume that the person agrees with them on important and relevant matters.

A University of Michigan study confirmed this. Early in the semester, researchers asked new students to make a list of the students they'd met and which ones they most liked.[25] At a later time, they were then asked which of the students they believed felt the same way they did about the important things in life.

When the researchers compared each student's two lists, the same names came up in response to the two questions. If a student liked someone, they automatically assumed that particular individual felt the same about significant matters in life.

Many participants in the study discovered that after they got to know the student better, the attitudes and principles of the individual they initially liked were not similar at all. Most often, the affinity then tapered off. The study proved that if you initially like someone, you are more apt to assume that your morals or values are similar. Once again, a Royal of high-quality morals who initially likes you will presume you have the same high standards. If there is no early evidence to the contrary, that is.

Integrity as Bait

In fact, a Royal will be much more apt to want to meet you if he or she believes your standards are high. That's one of the reasons you won't find many Princes or Princesses hanging around pickup bars.

What about finding an honorable mate online? Yes, it can be done.

I have a dear friend and business contact in a small town in Colorado who, for a very valid reason, was forced to divorce his wife a few years ago. Bill had loved her dearly, and it took him an agonizingly long time to recuperate. During that period, he devoted much of his time and his money to making sure that his ex-wife and daughters were financially well taken care of and still felt loved.

After a year or so, loneliness started to get to him, and with much apprehension, Bill decided he'd better get back into the dating scene. This was no picnic for a man in his late forties who had married his childhood sweetheart. Dating again was doubly difficult for Bill because he is the president of an audio publishing house and well known in his town. In addition, Bill is an ethical and intelligent man with high standards. Naturally, any woman he could love would have to be the same.

Since Bill isn't a party animal, he decided to go online to find female company. Bill is a champion at advertising his products. His first task in bringing out a new program is to create a profile of the intended buyer. He will then make a list of the "assets" and "benefits" that would appeal to that particular type of customer.

This strategy had always worked for him in business, so he decided to try it when he returned to the dating scene. Only this time, he was the "product." As was his habit, he created a profile of the intended buyer, in this case, "first-class" women. Then he set about making a list of his "assets" and "benefits" to such a woman. His advertising venue was one of the love dot-com websites.

Bill tried to be objective. He knew he was good looking, educated, articulate, accomplished, and wealthy and definitely had a lot of prestige. But now he faced the toughest advertising challenge in his career. He wanted to be modest yet present a truthful picture of himself.

"What the heck," he said, "I've always believed in truth in advertising." So he described himself as a "company owner" and "well off" in the self-advertisement he placed on a love dot-com site.

Unfortunately, Bill wasn't getting much response with his ad—at least not from the type of woman he wanted. It was obvious from the phone conversations he had with the respondents that they were mostly interested in his money.

There was one special blessing in Bill's life—he still had an excellent relationship with his oldest daughter, who was then eighteen. One evening when he was taking her to dinner, they were joking about "Dad's looking for love online." Bill disparagingly told her, "Alicia, I just don't think there any good women who read the ads out there."

"Sure there are, Dad," his daughter replied. Then she asked, "What does your ad say?"

He read her several that he'd run, and Alicia shook her head. "That's not what a woman wants. I mean, not the kind of woman you want." She continued, "Look, Dad, you're intelligent, kind, loving, and very respectful of women. Look at the way you've treated Mom and us. Why don't you list some of those qualities?"

Bill looked confused. He knew Alicia was right about his good qualities, but he didn't know where to begin. Alicia helped him write an ad that stressed some of his deeper qualities rather than his money and prestige.

The day after he placed this ad in cyberspace, responses started flowing in—"from much higher-caliber women," he said. A few weeks into his "advertising campaign," a very special "buyer" came along.

TECHNIQUE #39
STRUT YOUR GOOD STUFF RIGHT AWAY

Don't wait for Royals to gradually uncover your magnificence. Give them evidence of your good qualities right up front. Don't be embarrassed. It's crucial data for principled people.

So far he is still seeing her, and whenever I speak to Bill, he sounds happier than I've heard him in the past few years.

Girls Just Wanna Have Fun—Not!

Occasionally, men have asked me why women care so much about character and "all that stuff" so soon. They're confused why many women won't jump into an affair unless the guy passes the early tests of trustworthiness, character, sensitivity, responsiveness, and all the other definitions of a "good guy." It's puzzling because men and women grow up in the same general culture. So why is it that women are more apt to feel that love should come before sex, and most men feel just the opposite? In fact, many women need to fall in love before they'll even consider sex. And conversely, many men are only able to fall in love with a woman after they've had sex with her. Why is that?

The answer to that dizzying question lies in *evolutionary biology*. In what? Let me explain. It all goes back to a theory first proposed by Darwin in 1872.[26] He called it *sexual selection*. A psychologist named Robert Trivers carried Darwin's concept into contemporary society. He proved that—condoms, the pill, the diaphragm, the patch, and all other methods of contraception now known or hereafter developed aside—the female biological instinct reigns.

He put it in the context of the *biological costs* of pregnancy and childbirth. He said that a pregnant woman pays out a lot of biological assets—calcium, iron, vitamins (in other words, elements crucial to her health)—in the process. Conversely, biologically speaking, it costs the man practically nothing. Males produce only sperm to kick the whole process off.

OK, so the man may pay the bills, but the biological costs of pregnancy and childbirth are much more "expensive" for the female. She may look fine on the outside, but on the inside, that sperm and ovum can wreak havoc. I mean, you can't have another person starting to grow inside you without crowding your own body space and causing some hassles.

Then there's the matter of morning sickness. What's that like? Gentlemen, it's the same sensation as when you scarf down a seafood cocktail and a dozen raw eggs, followed by a Big Mac, a hot fudge sundae, and a six-pack of beer—and then you take a spin on the roller coaster. It's called *morning sickness*, but *morning* is a misnomer. The feeling lousy attacks come morning, noon, and night for about three months.

That's just the beginning. The last three months are the worst. Wouldn't your ego suffer a blast if you felt huge and ugly, waddled when you walked, and had to wear a tent? Not to mention going into sexual quarantine. If you don't believe it, fellas, put a cement block inside a beach ball and strap it to your stomach. Then try to have sex.

Then there is the woman's excruciating pain of childbirth. The male feels none of that. He ejaculates and his physical contribution to the project is over. And pain? No way. His whole contribution felt good. Real good.

In other words, it "costs" the female a whole lot more to have a child. Even if the chances of pregnancy are nil—say her potential lover has had a vasectomy—the concept of the biological costs are so embedded in her psyche that her sex-without-love reluctance remains. A woman knows, subconsciously if not consciously, that the major responsibility of rearing the child is hers. The intuitive fear is that if the man should disappear, she'd be left holding the baby and all the concomitant responsibilities. That's why she needs love. A woman wants to know that her man is going to stay around to help change the baby's diapers and pay for the college education.

Timothy Perper, who wrote a wonderful treatise on the biology of love, puts it in more erudite terms. He says, "Though men and women both treat sex as a powerful emotional cement, women's sexual hesitation has been, and in some ways still is, biosocially and bioeconomically functional."[27]

Many women, especially today when they often earn as much as or more than their potential partner, will choose to "invest their biological income" with a mate who is loving, honest, and responsive, no matter how much money he has. Men often think that women are gold diggers. Not so in most cases. To today's woman, positive qualities usually outweigh wealth.

That's good news for men who want to marry a Princess because it's often easier to work on your character than your bank account.

TECHNIQUE #40
GENTLEMEN, "RESPECT" SEX WITH A PRINCESS

Respect? That's an unusual word to go with sex. You might be tempted to say, "Sex? So what's the big deal?" Think twice. It is a big deal to a woman, especially a Princess. A wise woman is constantly on the lookout for clues to your character.

Your Home Is Not Your Castle—It's a Peek into Your Soul

Gentlemen, when a woman says she'd like to come see your home, don't get excited. It probably does not mean what you think and hope it means. It's a far cry from "coming up to see your etchings." For her, it's not just a visit to your pad; it's a reconnaissance mission about your character. Nothing will escape her eagle eyes.

Say she's coming over. You scramble around and throw all your dirty shirts on the floor of the closet, tell your scroungy socks to go run under the bed, and try to figure how that vacuum cleaner your mother gave you two birthdays ago works.

Your date arrives, and while you're going into the kitchen to get a couple beverages for the two of you, she'll sniff around like a drug-addicted German shepherd at the airport for clues to your personality.

At some point she'll probably want to use the bathroom. She doesn't need to go. She simply wants to peek into your medicine cabinet. What will she find? Will ten packs of condoms fall out? A cascade of Valium? Your other girlfriend's lip gloss and nail polish?

I suggest you take inventory of everything in your medicine chest, in your dresser, and under your bed. Then stash any incriminating evidence under your fishing tackle at the bottom of your closet. And if she's going to be spending any time alone at your place, even that's not safe. Bury it in the backyard.

I once was having a nightcap at a date's house. This "honorable" man had just been telling me how he hadn't had intimate relations with a woman in more than two years. He explained that intimacy was very important to him and he hadn't found "the one." That gave me the warm and fuzzies. I squeezed his hand sympathetically and told him I needed to use the bathroom.

As I entered his bedroom on the way to the bathroom, I glanced at his bed table. Eeek! I saw a pair of false eyelashes sticking to the side of it! Since eyelash glue doesn't hold very long, they were obviously just peeled off in the dark and placed there in the past night or two. It wouldn't take a fox to figure they were the residue from a recent passionate night. I wondered whether they were worn by a woman—or by him. Either of which, after his professed celibacy, stripped him of his Princely crown.

Gentlemen, to a woman, everything—even the type of toilet paper you buy—is a clue to your nature. Do you go for the more expensive soft plushy kind, or do you go for the cheapie kind that will scratch her sensitive tush? That tells her whether you're a generous guy or a spartan tightwad.

The Minute She Enters Your Office, She's Sherlock Holmes

Your office artifacts get the same scrutiny as your home. What photos do you have around your desk? Your kids from a previous marriage? ("Well, he did tell me about them," she's thinking. "But are they getting all his money in child support?") A photo of your kids and ex-wife? ("I smell trouble here.") Of your ex-girlfriend? ("Bigger trouble. Is she really 'ex'?") Of politicians or celebrities? ("I better look closer to make sure he's in the picture, too, or it's really strange.")

Be careful what calendar you have on the wall. That's a real litmus test for the little lady. Is it a Sierra Club calendar, an Arthur Andersen "for our valued clients" calendar, or a nude pinups calendar?

Forget about the fact that your office was decorated by the nut hired to do the whole firm and you had nothing to do with it. She'll still analyze how you've placed your furniture. Is your desk forming a barrier between yourself and any visitors? (She will say to herself, "He's insecure.") Is your space more open? ("Ah, he's more egalitarian.") Are the guest chairs just as comfortable as yours? ("Oh, good—he cares about people.") Did someone borrow the only chair you had in your office? ("He's a misanthropic hermit and everybody in the office probably hates him.")

It's not just the artifacts and layout she makes note of. She'll be judging everybody's reaction to and respect of you even as

Technique #41

Polish Your Pad to Reflect Your Principles

If you're happy waking up and looking into the vapid little eyes of a frog, don't sweat it over home and office. But if you want to kiss a Prince or Princess good morning every day, don't let your home or office show anything shoddy.

you walk past the cubicles. Do they smile, wave, and say, "Hi"? Do they instantly try to look busy? Do they avoid looking at you? Do they roll their eyes or say, "There that turkey goes again, showing off another woman"?

In short, gentlemen, unless you're boyfriend or husband material, forget having sex with your Princess.

"Who's talking about marriage?" you might ask. "What about a good old-fashioned roll in the hay?"

Doesn't usually work that way, fellas. Interesting thing about most women—their bodies only get as excited as their emotions. If they like and respect you, they're more apt to "put out," as some guys say. If they don't, you're the past before the present story of the two of you even begins.

Many men in my seminars have asked me, "Don't women really want to marry a rich man?" Fellas, it definitely doesn't hurt to be rich. But the world is rapidly changing. Women are earning more money. Women no longer need to marry a man for economic security. And here's a headline. Soon men are going to suffer a drastic woman shortage. It's official. A *Wall Street Journal* headline, "The Woman Shortage," broadcast the impending crisis for men. The article opened, "Thanks to a subtle demographic shift, men in their 30s and 40s are now fighting over a shrinking pool of women."[28] The tables have turned in the search for a mate.

What many men fail to realize is that most women are not gold diggers—at least in the sense of money. They want gold in their man, but a principled woman's definition of gold is being a good person.

A Word to Wise Women

To a man, things like a woman's character are not so immediately obvious. As long as a woman is, say, good looking and fun to be with, men might overlook a few minor character flaws early in the relationship. I repeat, "early in the relationship." When they start to get serious, their future mate's qualities become very important.

However, a man does want to enjoy activities or interests with "his" woman. Sisters, let's say your Royal Potential Mate has an esoteric interest in Tibetan spaniels or Montblanc pens. You'll certainly go up a few notches in his estimation if you let the insider's term "Tibby" for the pups gracefully roll off your tongue. Or when you mention how much you like the Montblanc Mozart or Noblesse Oblige line. These are the terms that aficionados in such esoteric circles toss around.

You already know I'm a great believer in the "fake it 'til you make it" philosophy of life. But beware! When you get into something that's really important to a Prince or Princess, it can get you in trouble. Royalty are usually much more discerning than frogs. And a lot less forgiving if your ruse is revealed.

Different Kinds of Similarities

There are many kinds of similarities. We've talked about how important it is, especially to a woman very early in the relationship, that you have parallel perceptions and a similar system of beliefs. Gentlemen, I've told you how a woman secretly dons a Sherlock Holmes cap, packs a magnifying glass in her purse, and slinks stealthily through all the twists and turns of your personality to unearth your basic character.

Women, because of this, your first dates are not as high pressure. Usually a man is not deeply exploring your character. He knows what he's interested in immediately—maybe before you've opened your mouth. And that is, quite simply, do you turn him on?

The second big determinant early in the relationship becomes quickly evident, perhaps in your first conversation. Especially for a man, it's your interests—what kinds of activities, hobbies, and sports do you enjoy? And do they match his? In other words, can the two of you have fun together, both in bed and out?

I repeat, this is *not* to say that a woman's character is not critical to a Prince, and this is *not* to say that a man's interests are not important to a Princess. It's just that women notice a man's character and men notice a woman's interests very quickly. It makes sense. By now it's common knowledge that women deepen relationships by talking together, whereas men bond by doing things together.

Fortunately for Huntresses, it's easier for them to display the kind of similarity that a man is interested in. In fact, I presented a thorough how-to in *How to Make Anyone Fall in Love with You*.

There are two problems with captivating someone by techniques, however. One, you will not be able to keep up the ruse forever. And two, a Prince is usually not only more perceptive than your average guy, but he's far less apt to be forgiving of any pretense on your part.

Fake It and You'll Break It

Let me tell you about a girlfriend of mine who loved and lost her Prince because she failed at her ploy. Several years ago I was visiting Barbara, another old school chum. She was just getting over a relationship with a wonderful man who fit her every definition of a Prince. Bernard, she told me, was "intelligent, rich, kind, and honorable." She said he "loved classical music and had a fine art collection and a vacation home in Tuscany." She said that when they were together, he'd told her that he enjoyed being with her more than any other woman he'd ever been with.

"So what went wrong?" I asked. After perhaps one too many glasses of wine, she confessed the whole thing. Practically in tears, she held up her thumb and forefinger close together and said, "I came this close to having Bernard propose." Barbara's sad story went on for several hours, but let me give it to you in a nutshell.

I'd known Barbara for quite a few years, and I was aware that her favorite extracurricular activity was mall-crawling. "Here lies Barbara. She shopped 'til she dropped" will be engraved on her tombstone.

Like many women, Barbara was tired of the "dems and dose" guys she'd been dating. And she wasn't meeting any quality guys in TGIF or Kmart at the mall. So she decided to "go shopping" for a higher-quality man.

Barbara had heard that ballooning was a sport that drew interesting men. Many balloonists are also affluent since owning or renting a balloon isn't cheap. She decided to take action.

Good for Barbara. She found a local balloon instructor, and, not wanting to spend too much money, she offered to crew in return for lessons. For several weekends, Barbara worked with a chase crew, helping rig the equipment and following balloons on the ground to help the pilots pack everything and bring it home again.

Soon her plan worked. She met Bernard, a pilot who was not only sportive and single but quite wealthy. Bernard was an excellent prospect.

Although she was new to the sport, Bernard adored the fact that Barbara seemed like such an avid novice in his sportive pas-

Technique #42

Be Real or Be Wretched

Your qualities had better be real, or you will suffer one of two sad consequences. One, as soon as the real you emerges, you will lose any principled person whom you've lied to. Or two, you'll pull it off but then be a gagged prisoner the rest of your life, forced to do things that are absolutely no fun at all. This is not recommended.

sion. They started going together, and every free moment, he took her for balloon rides and gave her lessons. When they went out to dinner, he would discuss their last flight and the wind and weather conditions for the next. He talked enthusiastically about Barbara getting her own balloon pilot certificate. (Secretly, that was the last thing Barbara wanted. After all, ballooning had fulfilled its intended purpose for her. She had found her Prince.)

However, it began to be a drag having to keep up the ruse about her love for the sport. Soon Barbara's laughter at Bernard's ballooning jokes began to sound less sincere. Her smile became frozen listening to stories about great ballooning champions. While her pilot-Prince enthusiastically spoke about their adventure the following weekend, her thoughts would wander. She'd be dreaming of her next mall-crawl.

Barbara's fear of the high-wind landings and the dangerous power lines she had heard about increased. Most of all, she got fed up with getting up in the wee hours of the morning, a dedicated balloonist's preferred launch time. Even the postflight champagne parties started giving her a headache.

Finally, one Thursday evening, Barbara told Bernard that she had no intention of ballooning with him that weekend because she hadn't been to the hairdresser in months. She added that she was long overdue for some shopping. Bernard was disappointed but didn't think much of it—until it continued happening again and again. While Barbara shopped, Bernard began ballooning with other friends. This left Barbara alone on weekends. They started seeing each other less and less.

Sadly, for Barbara, Bernard told her one evening that he had met someone new, an avid balloonist. Barbara was devastated and jealously asked to see a photo of her. When she saw that Bernard's new girlfriend was neither terribly attractive nor stylish, Barbara's resentment made her rudely comment on this fact. Bernard's response was that his new lady friend "preferred not to spend her money on clothes and beauty parlors but on ballooning." This was a great virtue in Bernard's eyes—one that Barbara had pretended to have at first.

The tragic bottom line for Barbara was that she had successfully faked it at first but discovered she could never make it for the long run. And when Bernard discovered she was faking it, he realized he could never make it with her for the long run.

Was it the lack of interest in ballooning or was it the lie that did her in? Probably both.

Barbara, of course, made a serious mistake even before she expressed her passion for ballooning. She should have looked at herself in the mirror and had a deep discussion. She should have asked the girl in the looking glass, "Do you really prefer risking life and limb up in the clouds to pigging out in the mall food court?"

Then she should have asked, "What is it that I enjoy that a potential Royal Mate would also enjoy?" Since Barbara enjoyed

> ## Technique #43
> ### Look for Like-Alikes
>
> Look for activities that you genuinely like that will also attract Royalty. You'll do much better in the long run that way.

shopping so much, she might have done better hunting for her dream mate by haunting some upscale auctions. Enjoying that, at least, wouldn't be a lie. And, shop-a-holic that she was, she could keep up the auction addiction.

What About "Opposites Attract"?

Hey, what about "opposites attract," you may well wonder. Yes, they do—to a point and for a short while. For a brief fling, opposites can be a blast. But practically never for a serious commitment like marriage.

Many years ago when I was a flight attendant for the now historical Pan Am, I flew with a lovely woman named Teresa. We always bid for the same flights, and I got to know her very well. Teresa came from a strict Catholic upbringing. In fact, for a while she wanted to be a nun. But when she decided the convent life was not for her, she took a very different path and become a *stew*, as we called ourselves in those days.

On a layover one rainy night in Liberia, Teresa told me she had a new boyfriend whom she couldn't wait for me to meet. She talked for hours about Ricardo. "He is a terrific dancer and a big partygoer. He can charm the knickers off anybody," she said blushingly.

When we got back to our home base, Teresa invited me over to her apartment to meet her new main squeeze. As I hugged her in her doorway, I looked over her shoulder—and there was Teresa's new heartthrob. I was dumbfounded. Not only did he not stand up to greet me, Ricardo remained reclining on the sofa, with one arm over the back of it, and didn't even look my way. This arrogant position revealed his half-bare chest, which was garnished with a tasteless array of gold chains. To top off the horror show, he was smoking a hand-rolled cigarette, which, to this day, I am not sure was tobacco.

The evening went from bad to worse as he told one witless joke after another. Fortunately, my sweet Teresa obviously didn't get some of the bluer ones. She sat there wide eyed and smiling like a little girl seeing Mickey Mouse for the first time. Teresa was obviously impressed with this male who was very different from any of the priests or parishioners she was used to.

I breathed a sigh of relief when on our next flight, Teresa told me that anything she said now about Ricardo would be in the past tense. She herself saw the reason for her temporary fascination. She acknowledged that, after her sheltered life, she was simply satisfying her craving for a short walk on the wild side.

Anyone who'd met Teresa and Ricardo when they were together would have said, "I guess opposites attract." They forgot to add, "for a short time."

Sometimes the Need for Similarity Is Crazy

Sometimes the need for similarity is almost perverse! The next time you hear one of your acquaintances crying the blues about being married to a neurotic, you have every right to be suspicious of your buddy. Psychoanalysts attest to the fact that neurotics are attracted to neurotics. In fact, the nuttier someone is, the nuttier the partner they wind up with. Stories about the "normal" woman who falls prey to a wacko, or vice versa, make great screenplays. But it doesn't happen that much in real life. Surely people do get involved with schizophrenics, pathological liars, and a wide assortment of other undesirables. But mostly it's folks with a little screw loose themselves.

Does all this sound unpolitically correct? My apologies—but I only speak the truth. A study called "The Relationship of Mental Health to Marital Choice and Courtship Progress" proved it for posterity. A well-known researcher gave psychological tests to ninety-nine couples who were either engaged or going steady. Each individual was examined on a myriad of psychological factors, such as their level of anxiety, the strength of their ego, and their amount of repression.

Six months later, the couples were questioned as to how their relationship was progressing. It was shown that the relationships

Technique #44

Be Genuine, or Be Gone

This UpDating refrain is more true here than anywhere else. A rich, creative, or gorgeous man or woman might marry someone who is not quite as rich, creative, or gorgeous. But a highly principled person will never settle for less. You want an honorable partner. Be one, be sane, and be genuine in every way.

of couples who were similar in their mental health rating had progressed much further than dissimilar couples, many of whom had split up. This was additional proof that like attracts like— even when it comes to a touch of crazy.

The salient point for Royalty seekers is that, likewise, very well-balanced and highly intelligent people will choose a partner who is equally bright and well balanced.

So what's the bottom line on getting an honorable mate? Quite simply, it is that you should become an ethical, good person yourself. Don't let one lie or one cheap move devalue you. And finally, make investments in your mental and physical health. Think only good thoughts and take good care of yourself physically.

How to Capture a Magical One-of-a-Kind Mate

Taming the X-Royal

Who is an X-Prince or X-Princess? An X-Royal Mate can be any type of marvelous mate with whatever highly personalized qualities you crave. Think hard. Who would you like to wake up next to tomorrow morning? Someone creative? Literary? Artistic? Someone educated, erudite, or wise? Someone extremely talented—maybe a musician, writer, performer, or celebrity?

Class-tracker Paul Fussell calls someone in this creative category an "X." He says, "Being an X person is like having much of the freedom and power of a top-out-of-sight upper class person but not necessarily the money. X-Royalty is a sort of 'un-monied aristocracy.'"[29]

Now this is not to be confused with the X-generation. There are X-Princes and X-Princesses of all ages. In fact, there are quite a few older Xs. Some would call them successful aging hippies.

Although an X-type Royal is not usually born to eccentric parents, he or she starts to show signs of X-hood quite early. A budding X-Royal is the kid who doesn't go along with the crowd. Rather than playing hopscotch or jumping rope with the other kids, he or she might sneak into the backyard to play with the birds—to paint them, film them, study them, make up stories about them, dance with them, or dissect them. This "little weirdo" kid grows into an artist, a filmmaker, a professor, a writer, a dancer, or a biologist. Curiosity and originality are the two qualities that motivate these unusual people. Passion is what keeps them going.

An overwhelming majority of Xs are self-employed because they are incapable of working for someone else or doing anything as mundane as punching a time clock. Some might even work at menial jobs to support their "craft," as they like to call it. Of course, if you ask them, "What do you do?" they would answer that they're a musician, an artist, or an actor. What they might not add is that they are a musician, an artist, or an actor who likes to pay the rent. Therefore, they are waiting tables or driving a cab to support their more creative pursuits.

An X is not born an X. He or she can come from extreme wealth or extreme poverty and can make a grand entrance into this world from either side of the tracks. As burgeoning Xs get older, they usually flee their parents and flock to the big cities to pursue their art or other creative work. Hoards of them flee from Easy Street, and just as many escape the inner-city slums. Most of them, however, are refugees from middle-class suburbs.

They are practically all educated, either formally or by themselves. Many have graduated summa cum laude from the school of hard knocks and have created an interesting life as deliverance from mediocrity. Most have brought themselves up by the bootstraps, which they have tied into artistic or unusual knots. You'll find many of them working with their hands—like sculpting, making unique crafts, or immersing themselves in a tub of oil paint and then walking on them across a canvas.

Then there are the celebrity Xs who choose to live an ostentatiously high-X lifestyle. These are the film stars, sports celebrities, or inventors whose crackpot creation hits big-time. I once went to a party at a congenial but coo-coo Italian-American artist's manor. He had built a canal running through each room. Dressed in black slacks, a striped shirt, and a white straw boater with a red ribbon fastened around its brim, he gave guests a gondola tour of his estate.

Tracking Down X-Royals in Their Natural Habitat

Using our location, location, location technique to capture an X is more difficult because, although many flock to art communities, plenty of them choose an alternative domicile. Some who are very rich try to hide it by choosing to dwell in the meatpacking section of town, a cabin in the woods, an abandoned church, or a homemade houseboat. If they do have a house, it's old, it's outrageously designy, or they've built it themselves. They like to position their abodes on the sides of mountains or on the tops of cliffs. *View*, not *security*, is their key word. If their home is self-built, it will consist of odd shapes like circles (geodesic domes) or triangles (A-frames). I once met an X who had a $300,000 tree house. Many opt for life abroad. Paris is a favorite X-destination, as are places like Karachi and Pago Pago.

Since many artist and writer X-Royals live in tiny garret apartments, they spend much of their time contemplating life and their navels in designer coffee shops. You'll see them staring blankly into space, pen in hand, eyes fuzzily focused on the cappuccino, frappuccino, and grande skim latte sign. Periodically they'll dive into the omnipresent notebook on the table. On that notebook may be the title of the next bestseller, the sketch of a painting that will sell for a million, a comedy routine that will have audiences rolling in the aisles, or the mad ramblings of a creative nut. They don't depend on their background or their looks or their money to get what they want. Talent is their trump card.

Besides coffee shops, good hunting grounds for an X-Royal are museums and antique stores. Also, neighborhood or ethnic restaurants are hot spots since many X either don't like to cook or never got around to mundane activities like buying pots and pans. Since many of these creative folks are home all day painting, composing, sculpting, writing, or meditating, they like to escape at night and go to bars or restaurants.

Where their bodies reside, however, is not critical. For them, it's the life of the mind. Xs are uninhibited, autonomous, inner-directed, and interesting. Above all, they are free. They may starve or make millions. They may be forgotten or become internationally acclaimed. For many, fame indeed is a goal—but the game is in living day to day with the liberty to follow their soul.

Many Xs reach great heights because they have overcome childhood challenges. The successful ones are shrewd and often get what they want through their ingenuity. Unless they're blessed with great looks or scads of money, they call on their creativity to capture the mate of their choice.

Xs Use Brains, Not Brawn, to Get What They Want

Let me tell you about the littlest X-Prince I know, about five feet four inches tall, who is also one of the biggest winners with women. My friend Jeff is a talented comedian who is asked to share his creative take on the corporate world with companies around the world. Jeff is short in height but tall in talent. He also has a big butt, but fortunately his brain far outweighs it. In fact, Jeff is something of a local celebrity.

He and I were having lunch a couple years ago when he told me that he and about twenty other men had been asked to participate in the Cancer Society's Bid for Bachelors. He said the other guys were pretty cool competition—a few football players, local luminaries, and an assortment of certified hunks.

I knew that Jeff wanted women to bid for him for two reasons. One, he believed deeply in the cancer cure cause, and the money went to charity. Two, he didn't want the humiliation of being the guy who got the fewest bids.

The rules of the auction decreed that he couldn't even talk to the women before the bidding. When I heard that all the women could do was see his picture and read a description of the "dream date" he would take them on, I didn't hold out much hope for him.

A couple of months went by and I didn't talk with Jeff. Then I ran into him at a speakers' convention. I hesitated to ask about what I figured had been a mortifying experience. However, curiosity got the better of me and I asked him, "Hey, Jeff, did you go through with that Cancer Society Bid for Bachelors thing?"

Jeff said, "Sure did."

"Tell me about it."

"Well," he said, "I was up against some pretty stiff competition. So I decided to use a basic marketing technique of carving off a market niche." He continued, "From past personal experience, about a third of the women I had dated over the years had cats. Those who had cats were fanatical about them. So I created a date package geared specifically to cat lovers.

"First my date and I would be picked up by a chauffeur-driven 'cat-o-lac,' which would take us to the zoo. There, in the Lion's Pavilion surrounded by exotic cats from around the world, we would have a candlelight dinner for two catered by a local restaurant called Katzingers. The centerpiece would be composed mainly of cattails and pussy willows.

"The limo would take us to the stage show *Cats*. On the way we would listen to music on tape from Cat Stevens, and she could keep the tape as a memento of the evening. Just in case the evening would be too much, I advertised that I had Dr. Myron Katz on standby at Grant Memorial to perform complimentary CAT scans. It was a cat lover's date come true."

A little more optimistic about the answer I'd get this time, I asked, "So how did you do?"

"I brought in the second largest bid for the evening. Mike Tomczak, quarterback for the Chicago Bears, came in first." When it comes to X-Royalty, creativity, humor, and brains beat a big bankroll every time.

Do Xs marry? Yes, but usually after they have lived with their partner for a few years and maybe even had little Xs—who, like their parents, wear only pure animal fabrics and never, ever sport T-shirts with bad jokes on them. Overall, depending on your viewpoint, they're pretty cool people. Life with one of them will never be dull—if you can take it!

Make Sure You Really Want an X-Royal

Now that you've gotten this far, if you are still convinced you want to love or marry X-Royalty, read on. But be prepared for a bumpy ride. You see, Xs will love you, but chances are their real passion in life is their work. Some elevate it to their calling.

There are some things you should know about X-Royals that will serve as a preface to your X-Royal hunting manual. Whatever tastes an X has, you can be sure he or she will go all the way with it. They enjoy going down unexplored, uncharted, and unprecedented paths. They can be engrossed by French billboards, seventeenth-century priestly vestments, the *I Ching*, or handicapped insects. And they are in a constant state of growth and change, not only in their interests but in their clothing and cuisine. One week they'll wear Tibetan robes, the next nothing but a kimono and happi coats. First they may be pigging out on Turkish or Indo-Chinese food, and next they're into 100 percent vegetarian, organic, or health food and wearing only natural hemp fabrics.

Then without warning, they may go ape one month and wear only "Made in the USA" garb and pig out on Big Macs, corn or chili dogs, Philly cheese steaks, Famous Amos cookies, and Key West key lime pie. Unlike honorable or high-class people, it's difficult to make generalizations about Xs because they are all so different. As is the case with any animal who doesn't like captivity, an X is usually pretty tough to capture.

For you, it all boils down to "How much difference can I take?" Everything is a little different about Xs. Many of them are loners. Because of this, some people are suspicious of their sexual preferences. But usually it's just because they haven't found the right partner who is up to their esoteric standards.

A Triple X-Rated Royal

Of course, like any kind of Prince or Princess, some Xs have such unorthodox sexual habits that it knocks them out of the desirable category for you. I once went out with an X I'd met at an art auction. He was impeccably dressed and extremely articulate, and he owned several art galleries in Newport, Rhode Island. As I soon discovered, however, nothing was "normal" about him, not even his name. His name was Caesar, which he pronounced "Chay-zhar-ray," like the original Latin.

On our first (and last) date, Chay-zhar-ray took me to a strange New York City restaurant where waitresses were dressed in black leather cat suits and stiletto heels. The waiters carried whips and wore black leather masks with eye slits so they could see. The busboys were seminaked men wearing chains and dog collars.

Partway through dinner, Chay-zhar-ray asked me if I was "into the scene."

"Oh, yes," I replied, choking on a chicken bone. I thought he was asking if I was enjoying the ambience of the restaurant. My answer seemed to please him—a little too much, I remember thinking. I attributed it to the fact that he wanted to make sure I was having a good time. His sensitivity warmed my heart.

During our dinner, he regaled me with explanations of impressionism, cubism, minimalism, and a myriad of other artistic styles, which I sort of half understood. After dinner, he invited me back to his place for coffee. Chay-zhar-ray had such exquisite taste in clothing and art that I was dying to see his apartment, which was on Park Avenue—an extremely prestigious address in New York.

As we entered the building, his doorman held open the heavy glass door covered by a network of cast iron. We rode up to the fifth floor in an elevator with shiny solid mahogany walls. Chay-zhar-ray looked especially interesting in the light of the elevator chandelier overhead. We then stepped into a foyer lit with a dizzying array of pin spots. When my eyes became used to the erratic lighting, I saw that each spot was aimed at an expensively framed photograph on the wall. Upon closer inspection, I saw they were bizarre photos of bold nude women standing tall and staring at the camera with a fearless and forthright expression on their faces.

"These are some of Helmut Newton's 'Big Nudes,'" he proudly informed me.

"Oh," I said.

As we entered his apartment, he was explaining that Newton's images were inspired by German police photos of terrorists and

Nazi propaganda imagery. I gulped and began to doubt the wisdom of my coming back to Chay-zhar-ray's pad for coffee.

I relaxed a little when I saw how beautifully he had furnished his sunken living room. We stepped down a few stairs onto an extraordinary carpet, "from Nepal," he informed me. He'd furnished the room as though it were a royal palace in Bangkok. I gasped in admiration of a superb teak sofa and Thai silk tapestries that adorned the walls. On a table were several carvings and sculptures. "They're from Buddhist temples, acquired on my last trip to Bangkok," he told me. I spotted one especially precious-looking piece, and, as though his mind was on other things, he mumbled that it was a piece of choice Sawankhalok pottery from the Sukhothai period.

As I was staring at it, wondering when and where and what the Sukhothai period was, he said, "Now I want to show you the red room."

"The red room?" I asked.

"Yes," he said, taking my hand and leading me down a long hall. At the end of it, he reached up under a small painting hanging on the wall just beside the door and extracted a key. He then reached into his pocket and pulled out another key. He fit both keys into two locks, like unlocking a vault box at a bank. He smiled at me, rather menacingly, I remember thinking, and turned them simultaneously in the lock. The heavy door opened. He reached in and flipped a switch. Suddenly the sound of Gregorian chants filled the room. A dim diffused red light gradually increased in intensity so that I could almost make out what was in the room.

Chay-zhar-ray said in a throaty voice, "Why don't you make yourself at home while I go shower and change into my chaps."

"Your what?" I gasped.

Chay-zhar-ray winked. "You did tell me you were into the scene, didn't you? We'll soon find out how deeply. And don't worry, the chamber is soundproof. I'm going to take my enema now," he added as he scurried down the hall.

"Your what?" I garbled, wondering what that had to do with anything—and why he tastelessly mentioned such a private activity.

I quickly looked around the room and couldn't believe my eyes, which, by now, were accustomed to the dim lighting. The wallpaper wasn't paper at all but red velvet. Hanging on brass hooks all around the room was an expensive-looking collection of leather whips, exotically shaped chains, paddles, and blindfolds. Right in the center there was a massive piece of wood, stocks it seemed, with a hole for the victim's head and two feet.

Now I won't feign that I was totally naive about this stuff. I knew lovers could have innocent fun tying each other up to chairs, bedposts, Nautilus machines, and occasionally drainpipes for their mutual pleasure. But Chay-zhar-ray's investment in time, money, interior decorating, and energy in his depravity was a bit too much for my taste.

When I spotted the beveled glass case displaying a collection of marble, wood, and exaggeratedly large rubber reproductions of part of the male anatomy, that was it. I decided I'd better leave— like greased lightning. I had time for a quick prayer as I bolted back to the foyer: "Please, God, don't let him have a padlock on the elevator."

Lest there be any misunderstanding, Chay-zhar-ray's definition of a romantic evening was not typical. X's sexual taste is usually as vanilla as any other kind of Prince or Princess's. However, do be prepared because Xs enjoy copulating in creative ways in unusual places—such as bracing themselves in a kayak, doggie style on a bear rug in front of the fireplace, or standing in airplane lavatories. If they do prefer traditional sex, it will most probably not be on a traditional bed. Expect either a loft bed, a hammock, a rubber pool flotation device, or a feng shui bed—for maximum Chi energy, of course. Or a room-size mattress on the floor to sleep eight people and one Doberman. If your X-Royal's bed does have a frame, it's usually brass, an old-fashioned four-poster, or homemade out of Coca-Cola cans.

Additionally, you'll never find a television at the foot of their sleeping spot. They have better things to do in bed than watch the tube—unless their preference runs to unique videos.

Incidentally, in your first conversation with an X, don't mention any TV show that you've seen unless it's a National Educational Television special or coverage of the latest national disaster. Definitely don't bring up any sports transmission.

In fact, many Xs have no TV at all. And if they do, they seldom watch it. They'll pretend not to know the meaning of the word *sitcom*. Unless, of course, they're analyzing a vintage "I Love Lucy" or "Jackie Gleason" show for the period mores, the comic timing, and so forth.

So, if this is your taste (and, I must admit, I'm kind of partial to it), here is your hunting manual.

Be Yourself, Your Most Interesting Self

Here's the answer to how to catch an X-Royal. Simply be yourself, your most interesting self. And have total confidence in your own intellect and taste.

Your living space should reflect your uniqueness. How should you furnish your home? Just like they do, which is "any-which-a-way." You will find no harmonizing colors; no matching materials; and no sets of furniture, dishes, or glasses. Everything in an X's home is one of a kind. Including the X him- or herself.

So go ahead, deck your pad with whatever strikes your fancy—a maze of neon flashing lights or a collection of Greek

Tᴇᴄʜɴɪϙᴜᴇ #45

Tʜɪɴᴋ, "I'ᴍ OK, Yᴏᴜ'ʀᴇ OK"

To captivate an X, give off an air of assurance that everything is precisely as you want it, in your domicile and in your head. No apologies for anything. Not for dirty dishes in the sink or a half-million-dollar vase used as a door jam. Have no hesitation about displaying a flower box filled with magnolias or marijuana. Oops, you left a garter belt hanging on the chandelier from your bacchanal the night before? No matter. No embarrassment. No blushing.

statues of nudes of all sizes and sexes. Just make sure it's nothing that can be found in a catalog—unless it's the Museum of Modern Art. Your living space can be as cluttered as an antique furniture store or as barren as a barn. Everything in the room should "tell a story."

Before the first time your X visits your pad, practice lines like, "Oh, that's a little something I picked up in Tibet." Or, "Oh, that's from Lubang Island in the Philippines." Or perhaps, "That? Oh, I picked that up on Prinzapolka beach in Nicaragua."

What's the bottom line on catching an original Prince or Princess? Simple yet complex. Just be curious about life and creative in living it. Do your thing, whatever it is—and do it passionately. Be sanguine and secure about your beliefs, your activities, and your life. If people don't accept it, the hell with them. You are intellectually, spiritually, and creatively confident.

A dear friend named Kimberly Ventus-Darks, a motivatio. speaker and one of the most inspiring X-Princesses I know, summed it up well. In a beautiful haunting voice, she sings to her audiences, "Live every moment of your life. Live it full and free." And do so with confidence and flair.

Ah, we come back to it, the most important ingredient to capturing a Royal Mate: *self-confidence*.

7 The Crucial Confidence Factor

Self-Concept Is Everything

Now, before continuing with your game plan, let's back up for a moment and make sure you're really ready for big-game hunting. "What do you mean?" you might well ask. "Obviously, I want to start UpDating to find a better quality mate."

Yes, consciously you may be committed to finding someone better than the frogs you've been fraternizing with. Consciously, you may feel you deserve "better." Consciously, you may have the courage to go out and bag big game. But human beings are wired in a funny way. New studies show that we make instinctive moves and have emotional reactions that have little to do with the brain.

Say it's the first of April, a dark night, and you're riding up in an elevator to see a buddy or a boyfriend. As the door opens, a chilling scene confronts you. A menacing man with a nylon stocking stretched over his face has a butcher knife in his raised fist pointed directly at you. What do you do? Your heart leaps into your throat and your stomach collapses on your colon—which feels like it's going to empty right there on the floor. Your knees turn to jelly and you scream. Then your sadistic friend pulls the stocking off his head, lowers the knife, and says, "April Fools' Day!"

When first spotting him, did you consciously think, "Oh, c'mon, I know that's just my friend [who, after that trick, may have disqualified himself from that cherished category] playing an April Fools' trick on me?" No—instead, instinct took over and you reacted accordingly.

Instinct also takes over during partner pursuit. You're at a party and you spot the man or woman of your dreams. He or she looks witty and wise and wonderful. But unfortunately, your potential mate is surrounded by a swarm of swooning supplicants. Is your instinctive reaction to join the throng, confident that you can win this prized person away from them? Probably not.

At this point, many wanna-be UpDaters are blown away with a bout of insecurity. Instinctively, to reaffirm their desirability, they turn to the nearest available lonely-looking frog whom they know they can impress. This unworthy person you've just met makes it clear that he or she wants to go out with you. You make a date with the admiring amphibian, and there you go once more. History repeats itself. Back into the frog pond—again.

However, if you truly and subconsciously are convinced you deserve a better mate, the story has a happier ending. You charge right into the crowd, fully confident that your magnetism will attract the Royal away from the drooling masses. Or you instinctively plot your subversive attack and go into swift action the minute he or she is momentarily alone. Due to your complete confidence, you are sure your scheme will work and you escape with his or her treasured heart. But alas, if you are less than confident, you only dream.

Fable? No. Fact—proven by a study called "The Effect of Perceived Liking on Interpersonal Attraction."[30] In this study, researchers rated 752 subjects on their appearance, personality, and intelligence. At about the same time, each member of the control group filled out a questionnaire rating their own desirability as a date, using similar criteria. The researchers were astonished when they discovered that their objective ranking bore little resemblance to the subjects' own perception of themselves. In other words, people have no idea of how attractive and interesting they are to other people.

A few weeks later and, supposedly unrelated to the first part of the study, researchers asked each woman, "What are the qualities you would want in a desirable date?" The researchers then compared their self-assessment and the desired-date assessment.

As assumed, the more sociably desirable the person considered him- or herself to be, the better date they thought they could get. They believed they could entice a mate who excelled in the same categories. In other words, people who thought they were good

TECHNIQUE #46
REALIZE THAT NARCISSISM NEVER HURTS

Remember all those bad things you used to call some people? "Vain," "egotistic," "snobby," "stuck-up." Not nice, right? Well, when pursuing Royalty, a pinch of pride is necessary. It bears repeating because, proven beyond all reasonable doubt, the more you think of yourself, the "better" partner you'll get.

looking assumed they could get a good-looking date, subjects who considered themselves very bright thought they could get an equally intelligent date, and so on.

At the end of the experiment, the researchers gave a big bash to which all the participants, male and female, were invited. Little did the revelers know that this was still part of the experiment. The researchers wanted to see who wound up with whom. Sure enough, the more the participants thought of themselves (whether their self-judgments were accurate or not), the more objectively desirable a partner they got.

Six months later, the researchers resurveyed the subjects. A good number of them were still dating the partner they'd found at the dance. Thus their hypothesis, called the *level of aspiration theory*, was proven.

Yet another study in a professional journal confirmed the level of aspiration theory. I quote: "A proposal of marriage in our society tends to be the way in which a man sums up his social attributes and suggests to a woman that hers are not so much better as to preclude a merger or partnership."[31]

This, of course, is true of both genders. It works both ways.

Self-Confidence Reigns in the Royal's Kingdom

In fact, when all is said and done, the absolutely most important quality for attracting and keeping an honorable, a rich or high-class, a gorgeous, or a creative person is self-confidence. Not conceited self-confidence. Not smug self-confidence. Certainly not conspicuous self-confidence. But quiet self-confidence. You must have a private and deep assurance that you are inwardly and outwardly a beautiful person who deserves a terrific mate. And when you make your partner feel he or she is the best, you have sown the seeds for lasting love.

No need to take just my word for it. Two of the world's most respected researchers of interpersonal attraction have conducted many dozens of controlled studies. All the investigations point to the irrefutable truth. They conclude the qualities that make someone fall in love with you—including the externals—all rank behind self-confidence. It's been proven that ahead of good looks, money, personality, and all the other draws, what matters most is being relaxed, having quiet confidence.[32]

That means you could be drop-dead gorgeous, be rolling in dough, be sharp as a blade of sunlight, and have 24-karat morals, but without confidence, your chances of capturing a Prince or Princess can shrivel to merely a wishful look in your eye. Without self-assurance, you might not even meet your Royal Mate.

You Don't Make the First Move

Without self-confidence, you'd be far less apt to approach your chosen dream date. After all, you figure, "He or she is so much more than I am, why would I even be considered?" Many of us come across as completely confident in most areas of our life. But when it comes to talking to an exciting prospect, we lose it. Suddenly, English becomes a second language. All incipient insecurities rear their ugly heads when we desperately want to make that good impression. It's a basic law of human nature: the higher the reward, the higher the reluctance to go after it. And finding a permanent partner is one of life's biggest accomplishments and rewards.

I've become good professional friends with a young woman who is my foreign rights book agent. Sophia is intelligent, fun, and absolutely gorgeous. When she's speaking with me or any of her colleagues, she comes across as insightful and assured. I can attest to the fact that she is also gracious and very witty. In short, guys would say, "Sophia is one cool chick."

In one of our business conversations, I happened to mention this chapter on confidence in *UpDating!* I guess this hit a hot button with her because she went ballistic! "Yikes, Leil," she said, "you are so right! It's horrible."

"What's horrible?" I asked, confused at her reaction.

"Being shy," she said.

"But you're not shy, Sophia."

"Not now. Not when it comes to people and things I know. But when it comes to guys, I mean a guy I like—that's a different story." She went on to tell me how, whenever she's at a party, she and her girlfriends will spot the coolest guy in the room. While they're all sneaking peeks at him, she said, "Some confident witch will walk right up to him. And, sure enough, they'll spend the rest of the time at the party together—and who knows what else after that. And all because I don't have the courage to approach a good-looking guy. If I'm not interested in him, then it's no sweat, but . . ."

In other words, Sophia has no problem being confident around frogs or her friends. It's the Princes who intimidate her. So who does a woman like that end up with? You're right—another frog who is definitely not worthy of her.

The problem is even worse for a man because, he feels, the only way he's going to meet a Princess is to either be introduced (but unless all his friends are in her league, he can dream on) or pick her up. Gentlemen, if you fear picking up a dynamite woman, you're not alone. At any given party, a full 99.99 percent of men look around a group and spot the best-looking woman in the room. Then they spend the rest of the evening conniving to meet her. They rehearse their opening line repeatedly. Just as they get up the courage to approach, she leaves with some other guy who moved in faster. Then they take it personally. They feel like a reject. But they didn't even talk with her! Why? Because they didn't have the confidence to make the move on her.

You Blow the Relationship

Even if you do form a relationship with a teriffic partner, without self-esteem, you can unconsciously muck up the relationship. Rob, a longtime friend of mine, is a remarkable and very handsome man. In fact, he's so good looking, I tease him that he could pose for the covers of Harlequin novels. His longish blonde hair and big shoulders make practically all female heads swivel when he walks by.

Rob never finished high school, but he was self-taught and is very artistic. He made a successful career for himself, working with leather making high-quality wallets and briefcases. In fact, he grew such a flourishing business that he now has a few dozen people working for him.

I once invited Rob to join me at a book-signing party for one of my girlfriends. At the party Rob spotted a fairly well-known writer. He commented to me he'd read several of her books and how much he liked them. Raquel was a spiritual writer. She was as beautiful as many of the concepts she wrote about in her books. She had attended the Sorbonne in Paris, and by all accounts, Raquel would qualify as a bona fide American Princess.

Rob and I were talking, but I could see he was preoccupied and entranced by Raquel. He kept furtively looking over all the while as he was telling me about how much he admired her work.

"Rob," I said, "don't tell me about how much you like her work. Go and tell her. Raquel is single, you know." Rob blushed and mumbled some self-deprecating comment.

"Don't be silly," I said. "She'd love to meet you." When I saw he was too shy to make the move, I took him by the hand and dragged him over to introduce them.

"Raquel," I said, "I'd like you to meet Rob. He was just telling me he's read practically all of your books and is a great fan of yours."

I could tell Raquel was impressed with Rob's good looks and demeanor. (We women have a smell for those things.) When they fell into lively conversation, I tastefully tiptoed away, keeping my fingers crossed that Rob would continue to get high scores in Raquel's book.

Indeed he did, and they started seeing each other. I was thrilled, and being the incurable relationship watcher that I am, I grilled him for details every time we spoke. Apparently things were going exceedingly well.

One Thursday evening a few months later, Rob called to tell me he and Raquel were going away that weekend. And the big news was that he was going to propose to her. He was in ecstasy because he had been able to captivate such a lovely woman. He loved her beauty, he loved her company, he loved her principles. He loved the idea of spending his life with Raquel. He told me he was hoping against hope she would accept.

"Me, too," I said.

Naturally, first thing Monday morning, I called Rob at his studio. "Well?" I asked.

"Uh, I'll call you later, Leil," he replied. It wouldn't take a fox to sense something had gone awry. Rob didn't call and didn't call. Friday afternoon came along and curiosity and concern about my friend was killing me. I decided to try again.

When Rob answered the phone, he sounded uncharacteristically somber. "Rob, did you pop the question?" I asked.

"No," he replied. And when I pressed, he told me the whole story in a voice as close to tears as a big boy like Rob would allow himself. Turns out, as much as Rob loved Raquel—and as much as he knew that love was reciprocated—he confessed he had always been uncomfortable when he was around Raquel's family and, as he put it, "her high-class friends" and all the "fancy parties" she took him to.

"But Rob, why? You're more charming, a lot more interesting, and for darn sure more good looking than any of them."

"Yeah, but they're all more educated than me. And they're all, well, classy. When we were together, I'd spend half the time worried I was picking up the wrong fork or mispronouncing something."

"That's no big deal," I assured him. "If she really loves you . . ."

"Oh, I think she did," Rob interrupted. In fact, he said that she even, lovingly and jokingly, referred to him as her "favorite and only student." She was trying to teach him, as she called it, "the king's English." Rob said he'd agreed to and even welcomed her corrections on his language.

"So?" I asked.

"Well," his voice started trailing off, "it's so ridiculous. Last Friday afternoon while we were driving to the lodge, I was telling her about a friend of mine who had sent us an invitation to a big bash he was throwing. In fact, I told her, 'He addressed it to you and I.'"

At that point, Rob said, Raquel, as was her habit, gently corrected him, saying, "You mean 'he addressed it to you and me.' 'Me' is the indirect object, and it's 'me,' not 'I.'"

Rob continued, "Leil, that's where I lost it. I said, 'Raquel, dammit, your big-deal friends are always inviting us to their hoity-toity parties. And I was telling you about the first classy party I can take both of us to, and you're crapping about my language!'

"Then I really blew it," Rob said, his voice cracking. "I started telling her how I was getting sick and tired of her 'snotty friends always looking down their noses at me.' I don't know what got into me, Leil. I guess it had all been piling up.

"Raquel told me her friends were not looking down their noses, and they thought I was really cool, but . . ." His voice trailed off, and he said he'd call me later.

Sadly, the story beneath the story was obvious. All along, Rob hadn't felt he measured up. He felt lucky to get Raquel, but deep down, he didn't feel worthy of her. He tried to be on her level but thought he wasn't, and it was obviously eating away at him. Instead of gently letting her know, it all welled up until he spit it out in one tasteless explosion. Thus he kiboshed the relationship by making it look like there was a bitter monster inside of him.

Rob and Raquel never arrived at the lodge. She quietly requested he take her home and has not returned his calls since.

Was it that Rob didn't measure up? Definitely not. As we explored earlier, their qualities evened out perfectly. He was handsome, enterprising, fairly rich, and witty. She was talented, educated, and had high status and prestige. In the Equity Scale, they could have been a good balance.

The problem? Rob's insecurity. Everything was going so well—until he irrevocably blew it due to his lack of confidence. If Rob had felt as worthy of Raquel as he was, he might now be sending out invitations to their wedding. What tragic consequences a lack of confidence can have!

When you have high self-esteem, you will simply assume a great partner will like you. As the clinicians say, "A person with high self-esteem will be more receptive to another's love than is an individual with lower self-esteem." Without confidence, you will assume the Royal will rebuff you.

You Won't Be Able to Love Your Royal Successfully

Another twist of irony is that if you do not have sufficient self-love, you will not be able to show your love for your wonderful partner in the right way. Often insecure people have a crying need for 100 percent reinforcement at all times. If they don't get it, they may, out of hurt, lash out and find themselves deprecating their Royal just the way Rob did. In other words, you may adore and worship your potential mate, but if you feel the least bit insecure, you can't show your love properly. Your Royal's love, in turn, can diminish.

This was demonstrated in a study called "The Effect of Perceived Liking on Interpersonal Attraction." When participants were told that a particular individual fancied them (even if it wasn't true), they wound up liking that "admirer" more than others in the group.[33] They chose to be with that person who was supposedly attracted to them. The opposite was also true. Unless we feel someone appreciates us, we're not so apt to want them.

Bottom line is, if insecurity keeps you from expressing your appreciation for a Royal, his or her love can dwindle. You *must* have quiet confidence to win the heart of a high-quality person. Without it, you won't even get to first base, let alone make a home run—or a home—with them.

We Know the Sickness—What's the Cure?

There are two ways to approach reestablishing your self-confidence. One starts with the inside and gradually works outward. The other starts with the outside and gradually seeps inward. Here's the first—starting from the inside. You don't need to cough up many thousands of dollars and invest them in psychiatric help. You don't need to lie on the psychologist's couch twice a week for a minimum of four or five years. There's a better way! It's faster, it's cheaper (like it doesn't cost anything), and it's often more effective.

Have you heard much about the mind-body connection? Essentially, it's whatever your mind thinks greatly affects your body. And whatever the body is doing greatly affects your thinking. This is not just some airy-fairy touchie-feelie far-out theory. It's been proven.

One widespread study of dental students revealed that exam time was the time students were most susceptible to colds. And the students for whom the test was most important or stressful caught the worst and longest colds. Their systems experienced the greatest droop in antibodies. Whereas those who were thoroughly confident about the exam or generally had a more easygoing attitude toward life didn't suffer one sniffle.

I witnessed this phenomenon of psychology affecting health firsthand. Once I was directing a production of *My Fair Lady* aboard a cruise ship. We were doing the Alaska run, and it was darn cold that season. None of us felt terrific after having been aboard the ship for almost fourteen weeks. But there weren't any understudies, and the show had to go on. Everyone remained hearty and healthy, belting out their songs and getting through every performance without a sneeze.

The last night after the final performance, however, right there at the farewell party, a few of the actors started sniffling. Several had to leave the closing night celebration early because of a headache.

The next day, we discovered upon disembarking that practically every one of us, myself included, had come down with either chills, a fever, the flu, the blues, a sore throat, fever blisters, or some combination of the above. And the star of our show, lovely little Eliza Doolittle, showed up in the exit lounge with an ugly mouth full of cold sores so big she'd get lipstick on her ears if she tried to cover them.

The actor who'd played Eliza's father, Alfred Doolittle, had thrown his back out packing the night before. The passengers waiting to disembark couldn't believe this hobbling actor had been onstage as Eliza's high-kicking father just the night before. The only smile we had that day was when he grabbed the microphone in the departure lounge and started singing not "Jes' get me to the church on time" but "Jes' get me to the hospital on time."

As the performers stumbled down the gangplank either convulsing with coughing, nursing runny noses, or frightening children with their bloodshot eyes or horrible blisters, no one would ever have suspected they were the glamorous onstage stars of the night before. The performers' minds hadn't given their bodies permission to crash until they took the final bow.

One of the most dramatic proofs of the mind and body being inseparable came in the 1980s at Tufts University medical school. Practitioners of mind-body medicine were able to convince any doubting new physicians by showing them a film. A patient was lying on his back with his head behind a sheet so he couldn't see his body. He happily sipped tea and chatted amiably with no feeling of what was happening on the other side of the sheet. Meanwhile, the surgeon incised the patient's chest, cracked the man's ribs, and was removing a lobe from his lungs. The man's mind had been hypnotized to not accept the excruciating pain.

It Works the Other Way, Too

Now that it's been shown that our mental state affects our physical being, we must realize the reverse is also true. Our physical being affects our mental state. When our body is standing tall and relaxed, free of tension, our eyes bright with a slight smile lighting up our face, we feel more confident. The lines disappear from our foreheads, we perspire less, and our heartbeat slows down.

This means stress-induced aches and incipient diseases don't feel comfortable in the healthy atmosphere, and they tend to disappear. And when stress dissipates, our self-esteem rises. Just like you couldn't keep a goldfish in an empty bowl without water or raise a Siberian husky in Miami, you can't house confidence in a stress-filled, tense body.

Here's a technique I call the *probing, pinpointing, purging* (or *triple-p) technique*:

- **Probing.** Several times a day, stop and freeze. Don't move a muscle. (Now obviously, if you are crossing the street, wait 'til you've reached the curb.) Are your shoulders scrunched? Don't move them. Are your eyebrows tense? Don't move them. Simply stay rigid in whatever position you are currently in. (If you're making love, forget this for the moment.) You have probed your body for the knots.

- **Pinpointing.** While "frozen," employ your powers of self-observation. Perform what I call your *body check*. Become fully aware of the position of every part of your body. Is your back hunched over? Are your shoulders tight? Is your head tilted to one side? Is one shoulder higher than the other? Is your face scrunched up? Are your hands clenched? These are tension points. Make a mental checklist to catch them all. You have pinpointed the tension knots.

- **Purging.** OK, once you've identified the tension points, you can move. Now start the "melting process." Concentrate on each tense part of your body individually. A knot in your left shoulder? Experience it. Relax it. Massage it if necessary to get the knot out. Then relax your shoulders. Let them fall to where there is no tension.

Take a deep breath and slowly exhale. As you do, let your arms and hands soften. Imagine those stress points as frozen rock-solid chunks of ice cream. Now sense those frozen Creamsicles warming up and softening into the consistency of soft pudding. Continue letting the icy chunks melt until they become liquid. Naturally, at this point, the melted tension obeys gravity and will begin to flow down through your body and into the ground beneath you. You have now purged the tension from your body.

Freezing and then making a few body modifications like this several dozen times a day can change your life because it opens the door to higher self-esteem. Not only that, but by virtue of having

> ## Technique #47
> ## Practice the Triple-P Technique
>
> At various times during the day, suddenly freeze. Then
> probe your body, pinpoint the tension points, and
> purge them. Try this technique at your home or
> workplace. Set an alarm to go off every fifteen minutes.
> Freeze and proceed as described. Repetition is habit,
> and soon you'll be in the habit of having a relaxed
> body—a place that insecurity and tension have a tough
> time getting into.

no tension, you will appear much better looking and more
approachable.

Be Careful What You Wish For (You Just Might Get It!)

Now it's time for a different type of exercise. Some call it "soul
searching." Others call it "a reality check." I just like to call it "asking yourself why."

"Why do I want a richer or classier mate? Why do I want a
better looking, more honorable, or more interesting mate?" The
answer is obvious. "Because it will make me happy." In fact, that's
why we do anything in life.

Why do you buy a better car? Because will it make you happier driving it, right?

Why do you buy a snazzy outfit? Because it will make you
happier wearing it, right?

Why do you move to a better apartment or house? Because it will make you happier living in it, right?

Wrong! At least not for long. New research has proven that we get used to things fast—real fast. And driving a better car, wearing cooler clothes, and living in a nicer place quickly become a "baseline." It's the little uppers above that baseline that give us happiness.

In the 1990s, a slew of top psychologists examined every twist and turn in the human psyche to discover what gives a person joy or grief. Surprisingly enough, they discovered that it's not your basic lifestyle that determines your emotional state. In other words, in the long run, you will not be happier with a richer mate than with a poorer one. You will not be happier with an attractive spouse than with a plain one. And you will not be happier with an imaginative mate than with one who's a bit more run-of-the-mill.

My first reaction when I read this was, "You've got to be kidding!" I was convinced that getting an awesome partner instead of an average one would make someone much happier. But a team of respected researchers led by Daniel Gilbert of Harvard found that people vastly overestimate the intensity and duration of their emotions. In other words, they soon get used to whatever they have.

If you believe that a great mate will make life perfect, think again! You may feel on top of the world as you walk down the aisle with your ideal partner. But the initial thrill soon wears off. Your life with Mr. or Ms. Longed-For will be far less exciting than you originally expected.

Conversely, if you marry your old childhood sweetheart who is equally as blessed with good looks, brains, or money as you are, you will be just as happy. In fact, probably happier because you have more in common.

Psychologists call the phenomenon of thinking you know how you'll feel about something "affective forecasting." They found it's even less accurate than weather forecasting! In fact, 99 percent of the time, people are way off base with what they predict will bring them happiness.

Suppose you marry a very rich mate. Soon, dining at the best restaurants and going to swanky parties becomes ho-hum. Soon all the fabulous clothes just pile up in your closet. And soon driving your Ferrari feels the same as driving your old Ford. In fact, you may become nostalgic about your old lifestyle. You might even miss hamburgers on the grill, donning your jeans, and jumping into your old "jalopy." As Tim Wilson, renowned psychologist at the University of Virginia, wrote in *Personality and Social Psychology Bulletin*:

> We don't realize how quickly we will adapt to a pleasurable event and make it the backdrop of our lives. When any event occurs to us, we make it ordinary. And through becoming ordinary, we lose our pleasure.

I had a grad-school college friend, a law school student, who dreamed of being an attorney, marrying a beautiful woman, and working for a prestigious law firm. Night after night for months, Richard studied for the bar exam. He could never join me and his other friends at the college hangout for a cheeseburger and a good chat because he always had his nose in his law books. (Frankly, we really didn't miss his company that much because all he talked about was torts and contracts.) Obviously Richard was obsessed with admission to the bar. He complained to me that he was living on a liquid diet, black coffee after black coffee, so he could stay up all night studying.

Finally the momentous day came, the big bad bar exam. "It was tough," he said, but he had high hopes. My friend held his breath for months for the results.

When the scores arrived, alas, he found out he had failed. Richard felt wretched. However, trooper that he was, he started the whole process over again. Once again, the big day came. And once again, he failed. Poor Richard. He sold his law books to a secondhand bookstore and decided he was a lifetime flop.

Cut to years later. I ran into Richard at a college homecoming week. He introduced me to his new wife and they excitedly told me how they were buying country houses, fixing them up, and selling them at a good profit. His wife was plain in appearance but far from plain in talent. She was the designer of the family—painting the houses, decorating them, and planting gorgeous gardens in the yards. Richard was the marketing man and negotiator to get the best price possible. He was extremely animated as he told me about their latest "fixer-upper."

Would Richard have been happier as an attorney going to his midtown law firm every day and arguing cases? Possibly, but highly doubtful. According to the recent findings, he would be just as happy as he is now, or just as sad as he is now.

Psychologists have discovered that what determines your emotions are little successes or failures and little moments—joyful

Technique #48
Remember, Ya Gotta Be One to Get One

The secret of UpDating? To catch a Prince or Princess, you've got to be one to get one. Depending on the type of Royal Mate you want to capture, you must be sensitive to all the peas we've discussed that might mistakenly brand you as someone "unworthy" of his or her superior heart.

ones or sad ones—within whatever lifestyle you acquire. The studies prove that, within reason, you will be just as happy doing whatever you do and marrying whomever you marry. Just as someone has a genetic predisposition toward obesity or a certain disease, he or she has a genetic predisposition toward happiness or sadness.

This is not to say, however, that we should not try for the best in everything we do. A Harvard researcher Daniel Gilbert says, "Maybe it's important for there to be carrots and sticks in the world, even if they are illusions. They keep us moving toward carrots and away from sticks."

Seeing Richard's face, I was sure he received as much pleasure from selling a house at a good profit as he would have from winning an important case. He enjoyed life in the country with his creative wife precisely as much as he would have enjoyed coming home each night to a raving beauty in an expensive high-rise.

But let's turn back the clock for a moment. Suppose that right after Richard failed the bar a second time, he kicked a dirty old bottle on the street in anger. Suddenly a genie leaped out of the bottle and said, "Richard, you are going to live in the countryside and make a living fixing up old houses and selling them." Knowing Richard, that would have made him suicidal. And then suppose the soothsaying apparition had said, "And, Richard, you will be extremely happy doing this."

"Fat chance!" would have been Richard's reaction, and he'd have smashed the bottle.

But the genie was right. Richard found happiness in a vastly different lifestyle. Our inability to forecast our happiness or sadness has a positive side. Sometimes something happens to us that we think will destroy our life forever, such as the death of someone close to us. This happened to me some years ago, when my beloved Ken was killed in an airplane accident. It was the most horrible experience I ever had and I thought I would never get over it. Today, it does bring me momentary sadness when I think about it. But it's not that often and not anywhere near the intensity I thought it would. I've gotten used to the fact that he is gone. Time is kind.

WHEN YOU GET WHAT YOU THINK YOU WANT (AND WISH YOU HADN'T!)

Conversely, many people do in fact get precisely what and whom they want. They are happy with their conquest—at first. Do you remember Shantral, the ex-hippie turned wealthy wife of the aristocratic Chaddwick? She is a perfect example. Her dreams of marrying a rich man came true.

But she soon discovered that having a full-time housekeeper, a gardener, and a cook gave her no pleasure. She thought she would be happy hanging with a classy crowd, but instead she never felt comfortable, not even with her new relatives. Poor Shantral became an alcoholic recluse. She had done a bad job, as most of us do, of "affective forecasting."

Hers is not an isolated case. I've had several friends who thought they were lucky indeed when they said "I do" to their dream partners. At this point, they wish they'd said "I don't" to marriage. Because now they're saying "I do" to divorce. Often we are blinded by someone's assets and we tend to overlook their flaws.

Many women make the same "money mistake" but never have the courage to go out on their own. Recently I gave a speech for a group of prestigious men, company presidents all, who had worked excruciatingly long hours to build their empires. After my speech, we had what is called a "dine-around." We visited one house for cocktails, another for appetizers, another for the fish course, another for . . . well, you get the idea. That evening I visited six lavish homes—and met six lonely and unhappy wives. I'm sure not one of them knew, as she walked down the aisle, that her groom would soon carry her across the doorstep of a gilded cage.

Men make a similar mistake. But more commonly, they are blinded by beauty instead of big bucks. Later they get burned by problems they hadn't anticipated. Arrogance, adultery, and lack of accomplishment are more common with phenomenally beautiful people. Being constantly admired feeds arrogance. Being continually pursued by men can result in adultery. Lack of accomplishment? Well, why try harder when everything comes so easily?

Fortunately, one of my friends bailed out in time before he married the beauty whose lavish lifestyle was doomed to make him uncomfortable. Rob was the handsome man who fashioned leather and fell for the artist with designer genes.

Perhaps unwittingly, his discomfort at being less educated detonated. You may remember that he blurted out, " 'Raquel, dammit, your big deal friends are always inviting us to their hoity-toity parties. I was telling you about the first classy party I can take both of us to, and you're crapping about my language."

Was Rob rude? Yes. Was Rob lucky? Definitely yes. He would probably have been wretched living a life he was not accustomed to.

I don't mean to say that all beautiful (Chapter 3) or rich (Chapter 4) people have hidden flaws. I merely want to warn you that you should dig deeper before saying "I do."

That's true also with extremely honorable (Chapter 5) or creative (Chapter 6) mates. Their lofty ideals may leave you feeling as low as a snake's belly. And creative people can make you feel as dull as a dog biscuit. All the studies prove that equal is best. No sociology researcher would place bets on an enduring relationship between partners whose qualities don't balance out.

> ## Technique # 49
> ## Do a Little Soul Searching
>
> What does that mean to us UpDaters? It means, search your soul and give yourself a reality check. Then if you truly want a "superior" partner, read on. If not, close the book now and realize you'll be just as happy (or sad) with whomever you get.

As I write, a song from the Rolling Stones reverberates in my head. They sang, "You can't always get what you want." But I realized that was not the problem. The problem is you can't always know what you want.

The Last Word

Do you remember the story of the Princess and the pea? I repeat it here because the capturing a wonderful mate metaphor is so similar.

> Once upon a time there was a Prince who wanted to marry a Princess—but only a real Princess would do. Hoards of women in the kingdom were pretenders and attempted to pass themselves off as a Princess. But he demanded the real thing. Our Prince traveled all over the world seeking a true Princess. Every time he thought he'd found one, she would do some dumb thing that gave her lower sta-

tus away. So the Prince would go home yet again, very lonely and sad.

One evening there was a terrible storm. Thunder and lightning crashed all around the castle, and the rain poured down in torrents. Suddenly, there was a knock at the castle door. The old Queen opened the door tentatively, and there stood a drenched and bedraggled young girl. Water was dripping from her hair and her clothes. Mud was oozing out of the soles of her shoes. She apologized for the intrusion and introduced herself as a Princess.

"Humph, we'll soon find that out," thought the suspicious old Queen, inviting her in. Saying nothing, the Queen proceeded to the guest bedroom, took all the bedding off the bedstead, and laid a tiny pea on the bed board. She then laboriously dragged twenty mattresses out of storage and piled them up on top of the pea. At the very top, she placed twenty-eight eiderdown quilts. This was where the self-proclaimed "Princess" was to sleep.

The next morning, the King, the Queen, and the Prince were sitting rested and refreshed around the breakfast table. The bleary-eyed "Princess" limped down the stairs. The Queen slyly asked her how she had slept.

"Oh, very badly!" the girl said apologetically. "I scarcely closed my eyes all night. Heaven only knows what was in the bed, but I was lying on something so hard, that I am black and blue all over my body."

Hooray! The King and Queen jumped up and started dancing. All the servants rejoiced, as did the handsome young Prince because he knew he had found his heart's desire. Nobody but a true Princess would be sensitive to the painful pea buried under twenty mattresses and twenty-eight eiderdown quilts. So the Prince took her for his wife, and they lived happily ever after.

And the pea? Well, that was put in a museum, where it may still be seen, if no one has stolen it.

Thus ends this Princess's story and yours begins. . . .

Your true Prince or Princess could be offended by any of the no-nos I've given you in *UpDating!*, as Hans Christian Andersen's Princess was to the painful pea under her mattress.

Regardless of your wealth, your beauty, or your background, disregarding even one of the arrows we've discussed could destroy the entire hunt for your royal prey. When you first meet your Prince or Princess

- One lie, one cheap move, one time not acting in accord with your principles can knock you out of the running with an honorable person.
- One copy of the *National Enquirer* on your table, a fur cover on your toilet seat, one pair of dice hanging from your rearview mirror can make a high-class person laugh you off.
- One mistimed compliment or swooning too soon for the wrong reasons can make a gorgeous individual turn away.
- One remark about hating your job or talking enthusiastically about a current popular sitcom can make a creative person instantly forget you.

- And a bad case of no self-confidence can mean the final curtain with all Princes and Princesses before the show even begins.

You are now armed with all the artillery you need to capture the heart of a Royal. And, not incidentally, by following all the advice herein, you have become an even better person.

I pray you find your Prince or Princess and live happily ever after.

 # Notes

1. Lieberman, David. 1997. *Instant Analysis.* New York: St. Martin's Press.

2. Graham, Dee, et al. 1995. "A Scale for Identifying Stockholm Syndrome Reactions in Young Dating Women." *Violence and Victims* 10(1):3–22.

3. Walster, Elaine, William G. Walster, and Ellen Berscheid. 1978. *Equity: Theory and Research.* Boston: Allyn and Bacon.

4. Walster, E., et al. 1965. "The Effect of Self Esteem on Romantic Liking." *Journal of Personality and Social Psychology* 1:184–87.

5. Bramel, D. 1969. "Interpersonal Attraction, Hostility and Perception." In Judson Mills (Ed.). *Experimental Social Psychology.* New York: Macmillan.

6. Moore, M. M. 1985. "Nonverbal Courtship Patterns in Women: Context and Consequences." *Ethnology and Sociobiology* 6:237–47.

7. *Journal of Personality and Social Psychology*, called "Half a Minute: Predicting Teacher Evaluations from Thin Slices of Nonverbal Behavior and Physical Attractiveness." 64(11):431.

8. Bossard, J. H. S. "Residential Propinquity as a Factor in Marriage Selection." *American Journal of Sociology* 38:219–24.

9. Zajonc, R. B. 1970. "Brainwash: Familiarity Breeds Contempt." *Psychology Today*.

10. Bossard, J. H. S. "Residential Propinquity as a Factor in Marriage Selection." *American Journal of Sociology* 38:219–24.

11. Walster, E., et al. 1966. "Importance of Physical Attractiveness in Dating Behavior." *Journal of Personality and Social Psychology* 4:508–16.

12. Major, Brenda, et al. 1984. "Physical Attractiveness and Self Esteem: Attributions for Praise from an Other Sex Evaluator." *Personality and Social Psychology Bulletin* 10(1):43–50.

13. Sigall, H., and D. Landy. 1973. "Radiating Beauty: The Effects of Having a Physically Attractive Partner on Person Perception." *Journal of Personality and Social Psychology* 28:218–24.

14. Hasart, Julie K., and Kevin L. Hutchinson. 1997. "The Effects of Eyeglasses on Perceptions of Interpersonal Attraction." *Journal of Social Behavior and Personality* 8(3):521–28.

15. Byrne, Donn. 1971. *The Attraction Paradigm.* New York: Academic Press.

16. Dickoff, H. 1961. "Reactions to Evaluations by Another Person as a Function of Self-Evaluation and the Interaction Context." Unpublished doctoral dissertation, Duke University.

17. Major, Brenda, et al. 1984. "Physical Attractiveness and Self Esteem: Attributions for Praise from an Other Sex Evaluator." *Personality and Social Psychology Bulletin* 10(1):43–50.

18. Blumberg, Paul. 1989. *The Predatory Society: Deception in the American Marketplace.* New York: Oxford University Press.

19. Malloy, T. E., A. Yarlas, R. K. Montvilo, and D. B. Sugarman. 1995. "Agreement and Accuracy in Children's Interpersonal Perceptions: A Social Relations Analysis." *Journal of Personality and Social Psychology* 67:692–702.

20. Fussell, Paul. 1983. *Class: A Guide Through the American Class System.* New York: Summit Books, pp. 194–97, with minor revisions by Robert Keel, 1999. (An earlier form of this was promulgated in 1935 by F. Stuart Chapin in his book *Contemporary American Institutions.*)

21. Ibid.

22. Ibid.

23. Lavrakas, J. 1975. "Female Preferences for Male Physiques." *Journal Research in Personality* 9:324–34.

24. Newcomb, T. M. 1961. *The Acquaintance Process.* New York: Holt, Rinehart and Winston.

25. Byrne, Donn. 1971. "Interpersonal Attraction and Attitude Similarity." *Journal of Abnormal Social Psychology* 62:713–15.

26. Darwin, Charles. 1874. *The Descent of Man and Selection in Relation to Sex* (revised ed.). Chicago: University of Chicago Press. (Originally published in 1872.)

27. Perper, Timothy. 1985. *Sex Signals: The Biology of Love.* Philadelphia: ISI Press.

28. *Wall Street Journal,* "The Woman Shortage," *7 Dec. 2002.*

29. Fussell, Paul. 1983. *Class: A Guide Through the American Class System.* New York: Summit Books.

30. Backman, C. W., and P. F. Secord. 1959. "The Effect of Perceived Liking on Interpersonal Attraction." *Human Relations* 12:379–84.

31. Backman, C. W. 1952. "On Cooling the Mark Out: Some Aspects of Adaptation to Failure." *Psychiatry* 15:451–63.

32. Hatfield, E., and W. Walster. 1978. *A New Look at Love.* Lanham, Maryland: University Press of America, p. vii.

33. Backman, C. W., and P. F. Secord. 1959. "The Effect of Perceived Liking on Interpersonal Attraction." *Human Relations* 12:379–84.

Index

About the Author

Leil Lowndes, internationally recognized communications expert, is a dynamic speaker and has presented programs in practically every major U.S. city. She has coached Fortune 500 executives on interpersonal communications and has conducted communications seminars for the U.S. Peace Corps, foreign governments, and major corporations. She is the author of five books, including the top-selling *How to Make Anyone Fall in Love with You* and *How to Talk to Anyone*.

Based in New York City, the author has lectured at dozens of universities and colleges, and has appeared on hundreds of television and radio programs.

Contact Leil

If you come across any communications techniques, send them to Leil so she can share them with others. She would love to hear from you. Her E-mail address is leil@greatcommunicating.com.

Sign Up for Leil's Free E-Zine

Would you like more love and communications techniques from Leil? Sign up for her complimentary monthly communications hint. Go to her website, lowndes.com and click on "subscribe."